Wrestling
with God

Wrestling with God

with

The Meditations of Richard Marius

Edited by Nancy Grisham Anderson

Foreword by Ralph Norman

The University of Tennessee Press / Knoxville

Copyright © 2006 by The University of Tennessee Press / Knoxville.
All Rights Reserved. Manufactured in the United States of America.
First Edition.

This book is printed on acid-free paper.

Library of Congress Cataloging-in-Publication Data

Marius, Richard.
Wrestling with God : the meditations of Richard Marius / edited by Nancy
Grisham Anderson.— 1st ed.
    p. cm.
Includes index.
ISBN 1-57233-457-6 (hardcover)
1. Meditations. I. Anderson, Nancy G., 1940– II. Title.
BV4811.M326 2006
242—dc22   2005025944

Dedicated to the memory of my father, Reverend Roy A. Grisham (1905–1991), who served as a minister in the Methodist church in north Mississippi for fifty years, including several years as a chaplain in the South Pacific in World War II

Contents

Foreword

Richard Marius:
Between the Curse and the Blessing

Ralph Norman

It used to happen, back in my bluebook-reading days, that on a late spring night at the end of term, after I had slogged through twenty or thirty turgid student essays and had not come across one which surrendered any slightest hint that its author had caught the main point, or even some secondary or tertiary point from my lectures, much less remembered anything of consequence about the great books we had spent the semester reading and discussing, I would stumble out to the kitchen looking for the solace of a left-over doughnut or cheese sandwich. Maybe I'd pour myself a badly needed and too long abjured glass of Scotch. Eventually, I knew, I would have to drag back into the study and face again the mounting evidence that I had wasted my life in the teaching game. Then a funny thing would happen. I would sit back down at my desk, open up another paper and, like Keats on first looking into Chapman's Homer, find that the world had changed. Every sentence in this next paper would be rigorous and lucid and graceful, and the ordeal of the evening would suddenly and strangely be justified. Night would have turned into day. The dark would have become light. I had been ready to concede that I was unrealistic in my expectations, and here in my hands was the work of a student who had gone beyond all expectation. She had not only got my point but on page after page was making points of her own that had never occurred to me. I would see for the first time what a first-rate paper for my own course might look like. The world of questions we had shared in class would come abruptly to life, large and luminous and gratifying. It wouldn't matter whether we agreed on many of the answers or even on the best way to put the questions. What mattered was that we two had been caught up within an argument that was bigger than either of us and would last longer, and would justify us both.

That's precisely what it is like for me now when after decades of disappointment and disgruntlement with the sermons I've been hearing and reading I turn to the meditations of Richard Marius, which Nancy Anderson has done us the service of tracking down and collecting. It's a slender enough collection, but considering the wealth of fiction and history Marius published in his lifetime, what the volume makes possible, as if it contained a code that unscrambled the larger and more familiar body of work, is that we begin to sense the amassing argument he was building in and through his own series of emergent occasions. Call them devotions, meditations, sermons, as you will; let's just note that each of them is directed straight at an audience that presumably has agreed to sit there and listen. It was never as if the members of his audiences had nothing better to do with themselves or as if Marius had nothing better to do than stand up and deliver these messages. Make no mistake; he is preaching, as they say in the field of homiletics, for conviction. He wants your soul, just as you are. Eventually, of course, he wants you better than you are.

So here I am, reminded of what it is that I have been dimly anticipating and missing all this time. I have yearned in a vague and sometimes desperate sort of way, depending on the occasion, to have words addressed to me in just this miserable and humdrum condition of mine so as to bring the Word to me, and here at last, thanks to Marius, something appears that sounds very much like the Word, but in an unexpected and perhaps unprecedented envelope of amplitude and generosity and good humor.

Now see, I say to myself, it has not been unreasonable to hope that when I read or listen to a sermon something more can happen than to have my mind parked in the "idle" position. I do not have to sit there with my foot on the brake, marking time the way I do when I stop for a long line of kindergarteners being shepherded across the street by one of those policewomen in orange raingear. Sweet children, no doubt, the Lord bless them every one, but it's an adult enterprise, this business of listening to Marius, and I will have to summon more than the usual fifteen minutes of forbearance from down in my pew if I am going to hear him the way he clearly wants to be heard. I will need my wits about me and have at the ready everything I've ever learned or pondered or doubted about the faith of our fathers. I will need to run and hold on fast if I want to get in on the argument.

There are four distinctive elements in this preaching. First, as in good Baptist tradition, he has taken a text, usually a quite difficult text out of Scripture, and he has connected it to several apparently ordinary events in his own life. But second, these are seldom merely ordinary events. Marius has been alive and alert in tumultuous times, and no single meditation ignores the shape of the larger public life. We may be hearing what his Aunt Bert said about Jesus changing the water into alcohol-free grape juice, but it's a world and a moment that is densely threaded with talk, at once trivial and utterly profound. It's a textured reminiscence and evocation, always. Marius has not had to skim through a card file or thesaurus of preacherly anecdotes to find them. They are flesh of his (very worldly) flesh.

A third and absolutely critical feature is the way we are reminded, most often off-handedly, that we are not the first congregation or generation to try our hand at a connection between a difficult text or a hard saying out of Scripture and our present hearing of that text. Saints and scholars have been there before, over many centuries, and we hear from some of them. Never, though, in a solemn or ponderous way, as if Jerome or Luther or More had closed the case once and for all. Marius affords these considerable gentlemen the same courtesy and the same critical distance he affords his Aunt Bert on the miracle at Cana in Galilee. He's quizzical and loving and amused all at the same time. There's a pleasantly liturgical cast to this evocation of our spiritual antecedents. You might think for a moment that you are in a Roman or Anglican service, which of course you seldom are, not anywhere close. (The Sunday morning address to his scholarly brethren of the Thomas More Society in Mainz is as close as we get.) We may be surrounded, as Hebrews suggests, by a great cloud of witnesses, but watch your pocketbook.

All this looks easier than it is. Our preacher is a man who spent decades in the company of Thomas More and the church fathers, and with all manner of heresy. But there is no fancy show of erudition. Dazzling or getting dazzled is not what this is about. In these sermons both the novelist and the historian have ceded right of way to the plain speech of the preacher. And the preacher wears his learning ever so lightly. If we are to hear, and we do, about Anselm of Canterbury—the inventor of that most difficult and elusive and tantalizing of theological arguments, the ontological one—we find Anselm being slipped gently and without offense right into the middle of a reflection about modern disbelief. Whole libraries and intellectual careers are packed and presupposed within the soft elision and easy aside with which Marius invites Anselm into his discussion. And it's not a cheap shot. It's not a piece of name-dropping. The use Marius makes of Anselm is entirely respectable and credible. You can take issue with this use, but that only means that you have accepted an invitation to become part of an old and important and ongoing conversation. You are caught up within an argument that is greater than either of you. If this is not what they mean in homiletics by preaching for conviction, it is something better.

Which brings us quite conspicuously to the fourth and most easily misunderstood element in Marius's preaching. It's what makes him sound at once skeptical and agnostic and inconsistent. His refusal to make the text easier than it is, or make its application to our experience a matter of foregone and conventional agreement, his constant invitation simply to ponder, or disagree, on the profoundest questions of belief and disbelief, his dismissal of the seers and sayers who hawk certainties where there is no certainty, put us in mind of Tillich's search for the "God above God." The first baptism and duty of persons of faith, it may be, is to be disciplined and cleansed by doubt. But Marius's acquaintance with sermons, like ours, was almost entirely a story of preachers embarrassed by doubt. The novels are studded with bravado preachments intended to paint over this embarrassment. Preachers in these stories are almost uniformly either mendacious or silly, and the average reader is likely to be puzzled by so much immoderation in the scorn with which such figures are depicted. The only exception is the Reverend Arcenaux's funeral sermon for a young suicide in *An Affair of Honor,* where the text is Psalm 139 ("Lord, thou has searched me and known me . . .") and the stark, simple message is, we do not know why God has allowed this calamity, and we don't even know whether there is a why. The sermon is of course fictional and not in the author's voice, but it was quite rightly read aloud by the distinguished Dean Emeritus of Harvard Divinity School at Marius's memorial in Cambridge, and Nancy Anderson has rightly included it here.

What shall we make of these transgressions of the conventional line fixed between preaching and poesy? Kierkegaard used to complain that in the "Christendom" of his day people expected to be edified and instructed at the theater while they demanded to be amused and entertained by the sermons they heard in church. They had it all backwards. They lived, he thought, within a confusion of the aesthetic and the religious. Kierkegaard had done all he could to keep these stages on life's way, as he called his several alternative ways of reading and being in the world, sharp, separate, and distinct. He had first come to the amused attention of his fellow Danes as Mr. Either/Or, and he would go to his grave fearful that posterity would collapse these and other carefully wrought categories into one vast and merely fascinating entertainment. He would, he feared, be denied his distinction between poesy and preaching, and nobody could in his view aim to become a Christian who did not know how to mind the difference.

It was not a danger peculiar to Copenhagen or to the nineteenth century. Across the water in London, over two hundred years earlier, poesy and preaching had come together in the spectacular performances of John Donne, who as Dean of St. Paul's commanded capacity congregations that might typically include the royal family, the Archbishop of Canterbury, scientific worthies of the stature of Francis Bacon, and a steady representation of emissaries from abroad. One Dutch diplomat is said to have noted "the wealth of his unequalled wit, and yet more incomparable eloquence in the pulpit" (Gill 5).

We have some of John Donne's sermons preached in younger and humbler days, such as the one he preached in the spring of 1618 as Divinity Reader for the students of law at Lincoln's Inn. The texture of this sermon, like that of most of Marius's sermons at Appleton Chapel at Harvard, is rather more personal and perhaps more confessional than those Donne would deliver later to England's highest and mightiest. Donne begins with an image that ignores at the outset any qualms we might entertain about mixing matters of taste and matters of conscience:

> Almost every man hath his Appetite, and his tast disposed to some kind of meates rather then others; He knows that dish he would choose, for his first, and for his second course. We have often the same disposition in our spirituall Diet; a man may have a peculiar love towards such or such a book of Scripture, and in such an affection, I acknowledge, that my spirituall appetite carries me still, upon the Psalms of David, for a first course, for the scriptures of the Old Testament, and upon the Epistles of Saint Paul, for a second course, for the New; and my meditations even fore these pub-like exercises to Gods Church, return oftenest to these two. For, as a heavy entertainer offers to others, the meat which he loves best himself, so do I oftenest present to God's people, in these Congregations, the meditations which I feed upon at home, in these two Scriptures. If a man be asked a reason why he loves one meat better than another, where all are equally good, (as the books of Scripture

are) he will at least, find a reason in some good example, that
he sees some man of good tast, and temperate withal, so do:
And for my Diet, I have Saint Augustine's proclamation, that he
loved the Book of Psalms, and Saint Chrysostomes, that he
loved Saint Paul's Epistles, with a particular devotion. (Gill 35)

But there are other reasons, says Donne, than saintly examples.

God gives us, not only that which is merely necessary, but that
which is convenient too; he doth not only feed us, but feed us
with marrow, and with fatnesses; he giveth us our instruction
in cheerfull forms, not in a sowre, and sullen, and angry, and
unacceptable way, but cheerfully, in Psalms. (Gill 36)

My guess is that Marius sided with Donne against Kierkegaard, just
as, finally, he sided with More against Luther. He loved slipping
through the horns of the dilemmas posed by the fire-eaters.

* * *

In what he attests is the only sermon he has ever preached or ever
will preach, a sermon delivered in Chapel at Kings College, Cambridge, on September 24, 1986, a sermon entitled "The Uses of
Error," the literary critic Frank Kermode remarks that the reading,
even the translation, of the Bible, which is from the first verses to
the last mottled with passages of enormous difficulty, represents a
history rich in misinterpretation (or perhaps dis-interpretation),
and that this long and apparently inevitable record of misreading
must be taken not as an embarrassment but as a treasure, or in
the parlance of this early part of the century, as money in the
bank (Kermode 425). The passage in Job, for instance, where Job's
wife, in the King James version, advises him to "curse God and
die": Among the many supposed renditions of that passage is a
sixteenth-century painting by Georges LaTour, in which a shadowy figure, a woman, stands looking down upon a frail, naked,
seated man. Is she advising him to curse God or to bless God? The
Hebrew can be read either way, and the Vulgate reads Job's wife's
words as a counsel to go ahead and die but to bless God first. Not

curse but bless. Most students of LaTour's painting have taken the woman to be hostile, even hateful, casting a scornful glance down upon the seated figure. But the work is untitled, and others have beheld a different scriptural scene entirely; it's the angel, they say, appearing to Joseph, bringing him explanations. The interpretation of Scripture, according to Kermode, is always like that. The Bible is uncommonly replete with invitations to "error" but error that has become fruitful and suggestive, and we can be thankful of the ongoing creativity and originality of what has been said or sung or painted or constructed in the wake of those mistakes. And so, as it turns out, in the immense yet somehow intimate space between curse and blessing, within this blasted Biblical tease lies . . . what? Well, surprise, a curse and blessing of our very own.

Troublesome passages of Scripture like these are the ones Marius liked to preach from. He took special delight and instruction in their deep-seated undecidability. Not for him the Sermon on the Mount, with its poor and its peacemakers, its hungry and thirsty who will one day see God and inherit the kingdom, its lilies of the field, and its eye upon the sparrow; nor parables, like the Prodigal Son and the Good Samaritan and the Laborers in the Vineyard, that carry with them their own conspicuous self-evidence and applicability. Nor does he turn to the admonitions of Paul, those recommendations of faith, hope, and charity that Paul addressed to the quarrelsome Corinthians, or Paul's recommendation to the faithful at Philippi that they empty themselves and like Christ take upon themselves the form of the servant. Not even Paul's explicit acknowledgement that now we see through a glass darkly but sooner or later face to face, or Paul's tortured confession in Romans, so crucial to the anguish of Martin Luther, that he cannot do the good that he would do and that the Law which was to have been a boon of righteousness has brought death and unrighteousness instead.

No, Marius preaches about Jacob wrestling with the angel and coming away lame and a bit off balance, carrying around an uncertain blessing and of course a more nearly certain curse. About Saul seeking out the witch at Endor in the haunted enterprise of discovering the doom hidden within his own kingship. About Jesus, arriving too late at the sickbed of Lazarus and weeping like any-body else who has ever looked upon the still cold face of a beloved friend. About Jesus the prestidigitator whose very first work of wonder is to make wine out of water for the guests at a country wedding. About Jesus bereft not only of followers like Judas and the unreliable Simon Peter, who was supposed to have been the Rock for the church which was to come, but also of the God and Father upon whom he had ever relied.

In the Library of America volume devoted to American ser-mons, a collection running from Robert Cushman's 1622 sermon "preached at Plimouth in Newe Englande" to April 3, 1968, the day on which Martin Luther King Jr. preached his last sermon, there are no entries, save one, exhibiting the fourfold amplitude we find in the collection before us. That one of course is the sav-ing one, in which King tells us he has been to the mountain and is not afraid to die. On its surface there is no skepticism, only affir-mation and certainty, no bravado, only bravery in its purest form. Marius would say, perhaps somewhere does say, that beneath the surface there surges a powerful groundswell of skepticism about America and its ideals. King was entitled to the freedom he brought to the pulpit that night in Memphis because he had been baptized in naysaying and harshly schooled in the most rigorous kind of doubt then known to his people.

On every page of the Anderson collection, Marius covets the same kind of freedom. It appears that at his death he had gone a long way toward earning it. Without question he has shown us what we ought to be listening for in preachments though he has not made the task of preaching any easier.

Works Cited

Gill, Theodore, ed. *The Sermons of John Donne*. New York: Penguin, 1983.

Kermode, Frank. *The Uses of Error*. Cambridge, MA: Harvard UP, 1991.

Warner, Michael, ed. *American Sermons* (Library of America Series 108). New York: Pilgrim Putnam, 1999.

Acknowledgments

I have had the support and encouragement of a number of people in collecting Richard Marius's sermons and meditations. Without them, *Wrestling with God* would not have been published.

Lanier Smythe, for her friendship and trust.

Richard Anderson, for his laughter and love and listening.

Bishop Paul A. Duffey, retired bishop of the United Methodist Church, for his reading and support.

Ralph Norman, for his invaluable contributions to this collection.

Ann Close, for her guardianship of Richard Marius's literary estate.

Mary Hicks, for the original transcriptions of the selections in this volume.

Fariba Deravi, for her advocacy for support of faculty research at Auburn University Montgomery.

The Kimbrough Faculty Sabbatical Endowment Fund, compliments of Quida and John Kimbrough, established to underwrite costs related to faculty research at Auburn University Montgomery.

The research that resulted in this book was partially supported by grants from the Auburn University Montgomery Research Grant-in-Aid Program.

Introduction

Nay in all that toil, that coil, since
        (seems) I kissed the rod,
Hand rather, my heart lo! lapped
        strength, stole joy, would
        laugh, chéer.
Cheer whom though? The Hero whose
        heaven-handling flung me,
        fóot tród
Me? or me that fought him? O which
        one? is it each one? That
        night, that year
Of now done darkness I wretch lay
        wrestling with (my God!) my
        God.
—Gerard Manley Hopkins, [Carrion
        Comfort]

Throughout his life Richard Marius wrestled with God.

Marius had, on the surface, a typical childhood for someone
reared in rural Tennessee—farm chores, church, school, playing

with three siblings. There were, however, at least two notable exceptions to that representative normality: his father and his older brother.

Unique to this setting was his father, a Greek immigrant to East Tennessee following World War I. After Henri S. Marius settled in the Knoxville–Lenoir City area as a chemist at the foundry for the railway, he met and married Eunice Henck, a native of that part of the state who was working as a journalist for a Knoxville newspaper. (Henri Marius's journey from Greece to Tennessee is the foundation of his son's third novel, *After the War,* in which the narrator, Paul Alexander, makes a similar journey.)

The Mariuses' first son, James, born in 1926 with Down syndrome, had two direct influences on his younger brother's life. To protect James from curiosity and intolerance, Mr. Marius moved his family from Knoxville to what had been a summer place near Martel, Tennessee, later known as Dixie Lee Junction. Growing up in this pastoral setting had a profound effect on Marius's childhood and his education. In an autobiographical narrative, "The Middle of the Journey" (*Sewanee Review,* Summer 1977: 460–67), Marius fondly recalls the rural isolation of his childhood as "dreamlike and unreal" with a "sense of tremendous space." It was a natural world of beauty and wonder as well as a world of harshness, filled with the terrors of storms, the reality of snakes and hog-killing, the monotony of chores. Worried about her children's isolation, Mrs. Marius read works of classic literature aloud— Twain, Kipling, Poe, Dickens. And every year she read the King James Version of the Bible all the way through to her children, instilling in her son the love of words and stories. In the autobiographical essay, Marius remembers the voice of his mother

> rising to the sublime cadences of the Old Testament by the fireplace on wintry nights when both the flames in the grate and the divine words worked to thrust back the cold dark that crept in from the woods outside. I recall the melody of those enthralling sentences in the summer mornings when beyond the open window at her head we could hear the singing of birds.

So Richard grew up loving the sounds and rhythms of words. In addition, his world was filled with storytellers, both members of the community and of his family: "My mother's people told stories and told them again and again. In their way the yarns were as formal as Japanese kabuki drama, but we never tired of them."

The other profound influence of Marius's older brother was his mother's plan for her second son's future: he grew up knowing that he was destined for the ministry. In "The Middle of the Journey," Marius says that his mother "believed that my older brother was a curse sent by God because she had not become a missionary." As a result of this "curse," Mrs. Marius promised her second-born son to God to atone for her sins. Richard Marius was that son, born in the summer of 1933, to a mother "cursed" by religion and a father who "generally held priests and preachers in contempt."

The daughter of a Methodist evangelist, Mrs. Marius took her family to the nearby Methodist church. However, after an Emory graduate serving the church as its preacher in the early 1940s told Mrs. Marius that Jesus had sinned or made mistakes, she left the Methodist church and took her children to the Midway Baptist Church, which later became Dixie Lee Baptist Church. On 15 May 1948, the church's handwritten minutes record the vote on the baptism and church membership of "Dickie" and "Johney" Marius. According to the minutes, the service accepting the two brothers was on 16 May. Richard Marius's brother John recalls the baptism as taking place on Sunday afternoon in a backwater of Fort Loudon Lake, probably at the end of a revival. Throughout his youth and young adult days, Richard Marius was an active member of this church, attending services on Sundays and on Wednesday nights and for the Saturday night hymn-singing, celebrations that resulted in his knowing all stanzas of most hymns. In the mid-1970s, while teaching at the University of Tennessee–Knoxville, Marius began attending a Unitarian church after speaking there one Sunday. When he moved to Belmont, Massachusetts, he went to the Unitarian church near his house and later attended Memorial Chapel at Harvard with his son John.

Marius attended public schools and, during high school and college, wrote for the *Lenoir City News*. He was a senior in high school when he decided to enter the ministry, accepting his mother's "destiny" for him. After graduation from Lenoir City

High School, he entered the University of Tennessee in Knoxville to major in journalism while continuing to work at the newspaper, living at home and hitchhiking into Knoxville for classes. In addition to the journalism job, according to the minutes of the church, he served as associate pastor, elected at a business session in May of 1952. The church accepted his resignation on 14 October 1953, early in his senior year at the university.

The first crisis of faith occurred during his first year at UTK in the form of a reading assignment for a freshman composition class: he read W. T. Stace's "Man Against Darkness," in which the author develops the thesis that "The world is just what it is, and that is the end of the inquiry. There is no reason for its being what it is. Everything might just as well have been quite different, and there would have been no reason for that either." Thus, the youth's childhood faith, inherited from his mother, confronted Stace's "meaningless" and "purposeless" universe. And so began Richard Marius's lifelong struggle to find meaning and purpose in his life and in his world.

Though shaken, Marius made a serious effort to prepare for the ministry by entering seminary. After graduation from UTK, he attended the New Orleans Baptist Theological Seminary for "one hellish year" (his words) during which he spent weekends preaching in Baptist churches, especially in Mississippi. (See the appendix for Marius's "Ruleville: Reminiscence, Reflection" on that year a decade later.) In 1955 he transferred to the Baptist seminary in Louisville, Kentucky, from which he received a B.D. in 1958, after spending 1956 at the University of Strasbourg in France on a Rotary Foundation Scholarship. The minutes of the Dixie Lee Baptist Church record his tenure as a "supply pastor" for a brief period in the fall of 1957. He also performed the wedding ceremony for his brother John and his wife, Phyllis, on 21 December 1958.

In the fall of 1958, Marius "blundered" into graduate work at Yale to study the ancient Near East because of his fascination with mythology. After realizing that he needed knowledge of more languages than French, Hebrew, and Greek, he shifted to Renaissance and Reformation history, completing his M.A. in 1959 and Ph.D. in 1962. During his years in graduate school he served as pastor at the Baptist church in New Milford, Connecticut, and became an editor on the Yale edition of the complete works of Thomas More. Even after his days as a graduate student at Yale, he continued his association with this undertaking and by the sixth volume, in 1982, was listed as a coeditor of the multivolume series, along with Thomas M. C. Lawler and Germain Marc'hadour. This work resulted in his biography of the saint, a 1984 American Book Award finalist.

With his doctoral degree in Renaissance and Reformation history, Marius decided to enter the academic field, serving first on the history faculty at Gettysburg College for two years and then returning to his alma mater in Knoxville, where he taught history for fourteen years. During that time back in Tennessee, writing gradually became an integral part of his life, both for his classroom and for his career. By the late 1970s he had become well known enough in the field of writing that he was offered the job of director of expository writing at Harvard University, a position he held from 1978 through 1994, at which time he returned to the classroom full time to teach writing and literature courses covering a diversity of subjects from William Shakespeare to William Faulkner. He retired in 1998 to devote his time to writing but died of pancreatic cancer late in 1999.

Despite his doubts and his failure to fulfill his mother's promise to God, the religious background of Richard Marius's youth and education remained fundamental to his professional and personal life. Friends and relatives recall that serious conversations with him always turned to faith, belief, and death. Also, in his four novels, he drew on these religious struggles and questions as driving forces in his fiction. In *The Coming of Rain* (1969), a mad and fanatical Baptist minister, believing God had predestined him to damnation, is a voice of doom to the small fictional community of Bourbonville, Tennessee, and a threat to the woman he hopes will save him. A character in *Bound for the Promised Land* (1976) explains to the protagonist her belief about whether there is any cause and effect in the events of her life or whether she is simply carrying out predestined actions: "we're merely chips on the flood. It's almost the same thing as predestination, isn't it? . . . Is the flood that carries us along directed by God? Is it going somewhere? Or is it just moving? And if things were different, would there be any reason for that?" Destiny, or fate, figures again in the ponderings of Paul Alexander, the narrator of *After the War* (1991), a novel loosely based on Henri Marius's journey from Greece to settle in East Tennessee at the end of World War I. In *An Affair of Honor* (2001), Paul's son Charles is torn between a fundamental faith and doubt introduced by Stace's meaningless universe. So, Marius's fictional creations ponder questions that plagued their creator: belief in God, predestination or free will, religious fanaticism, fate or destiny, cause and effect, meaning and purpose—or meaninglessness and purposelessness—in the universe.

Although Marius did not officially serve a church after his days of preaching during seminary and his graduate work at Yale, he frequently took to the pulpit. The selections in *Wrestling with God,* the result of his lifelong search for answers in his personal life as well as his fictional writings, span his career from the late 1950s to the last months before his death. With the exception of the eulogy excerpted from his last novel, *An Affair of Honor,* Marius delivered these meditations publicly, from the 1959 sermon to a Lenoir City congregation and the Christmas Eve message to his congregation at New Milford, Connecticut, during graduate school years, through numerous meditations at Harvard's Morning Prayers during his tenure at the university and the presentation at the Thomas More conference in Maynooth, Ireland, in 1998. A few of them have also been published, in the series of *Best Sermons* or by Harvard Divinity School.

Marius was a frequent speaker at Morning Prayers, a daily service in the Appleton Chapel of the Memorial Church at Harvard University designed to prepare the attendants for their day ahead and to pray for the community and the world at large. Each day's service follows the same order of worship: responsive reading, generally from the Psalms; an anthem or chants by members of the Harvard University Choir; a scripture reading by either the clergy on duty or the day's speaker; a three-to-five-minute talk (hence the brevity of many of these selections); a prayer followed by the Lord's Prayer; and a closing hymn. The majority of the meditations in *Wrestling with God* are messages Marius delivered at this service, dated and preserved as typescripts with numerous handwritten revisions, in a file marked "Morning Meditations."

In addition to texts of the meditations and sermons for special occasions such as "Finding God in Strange Places" for the service to dedicate an organ and "A Meditation on Time and Creation" for a Thomas More conference, Richard Marius kept copies of the many messages he wrote and delivered to commemorate marriages, birthdays, and retirements of friends. These joyous celebrations frequently include a serious thought, as in the verse marking the tenth anniversary of friends' marriage:

> Ten Years are long enough
> To summon up reflections
> In proper reverence to a serious time.
> A decade is a seventh part
> Of that three score and ten
> Allowed, the Psalmist sang, to be
> The years we can enjoy
> Before such days as may remain,
> He glumly but sublimely said,
> Become but toil and sorrow
> When we must shortly pass away.

Brief phrases in Marius's parodies of "The Raven" or "The Love Song of J. Alfred Prufrock," written for retirement parties, contain overtones of his more serious concerns: "the dark tomorrow in our existential sorrow" and "The passing seasons sing a hard refrain[;] / The days whirl by. . . ." Occasionally a course syllabus might remind students that "we find mysteries and tantalizing questions we cannot answer."

Marius's communications with his high-school classmates at Lenoir City High School concentrate on detailed shared memories but also grow melancholy for brief moments, especially when he ponders passage of time and deaths of friends. He recalls a "threatening world," where "Suddenly the [train] whistles were gone, leaving only a ghost of sound that comes back now like so many other ghosts to haunt us with the remembrance of things past and lost." Or in that unique blend of the serious and the light-hearted, he wishes that "God would waste less time helping the [Tennessee] Volunteers win football games and spend more time working on a cure for cancer."

Eulogies that Marius delivered for friends confront the meaning of life and death, most specifically speaking about this "fear-haunted society of ours [where] death throws a horror of darkness backwards over life." At one memorial service he said:

> I grew up in a Southern Baptist religious tradition that insisted on finding divine purpose in everything. . . . I long ago gave up such easy comforts. There is a wind that blows across the world from nowhere into silence. I think it far better and more comforting to bow to the unknown and unknowable mystery than to make easy pronouncements about what God might have on his mind by visiting calamities upon us. . . . And yet I cannot give up everything from that perdurable teaching about purpose. The purpose of things is not to be found in some easy reading of the secret counsels of God; it is to be found in what we make of what we see and know.

That statement sums up what seems to be Richard Marius's personal answer to what is the meaning and purpose of it all— "what we see and know"—family and friends, laughter, the beauty and cycles of nature, travel, and, perhaps, most of all, his writing. After all, as he told classmates at their thirtieth class reunion, "A good story makes us all immortal as long as the story is being told," a philosophy dramatized in *After the War.* In fact, he frequently told friends and interviewers that he wrote because he was going to die, that the stories were his bid for immortality.

Richard Marius's meditations and sermons ponder the same subjects inherent in his fiction and scholarly writings: the passage of time, the meaning and purpose of our world, the beauty of nature, the devastation of cancer, faith or belief, our responsibilities to each other, our friends and family. He articulated the doubt and his own response to it early in his writings, with the dark conclusion of his first biography of Martin Luther:

We turn from the study of Luther, the theologian of arcane lore about an arcane deity, knowing that there is no help for us but that residing in our own heads and hearts, confessing wryly, too, that that help is feeble enough. If there is anything else that his life can teach us, it may well be that all our striving, like his, must finally be hidden in the long cold that comes for great and small alike, and that life at its best and all history, too, are but parts of the process whereby we make our own terms with the dark. Perhaps he found the peace and hope he wished. (*Luther: A Biography* [1974])

And similarly he concluded his final meditation at Morning Prayers:

I do not believe in surrender to the inevitable. We wrestle in the dark with God almost every day. . . . We may emerge lame from the battle, but we may also win it, and it is a kind of victory if we make the struggle ours even if we lose.

A Note on Biographical Sources

During a friendship spanning nearly twenty years, Richard and I had many occasions to discuss writing, teaching writing, and books—by him and by others. As background for the essay on Richard for the *Dictionary of Literary Biography Yearbook 1985,* I did extensive reading in primary and secondary sources and have tried to keep up with both categories since the publication of that reference volume. From 1987 through 1996, I served as a member of the faculty for the Tennessee Governor's Academy for Teachers of Writing and attended Richard's institute on writing Tennessee history in 1990. After Richard's death in 1999, his widow, Lanier Smythe, gave me access to his personal library and papers (with some restrictions) prior to deposit in Special Collections at the University of Tennessee. On each of three research trips to Boston, I found copies of sermons and meditations, generally in typescript and often edited in Richard's handwriting.

Richard's brother John and his wife, Phyllis, have also shared reminiscences and provided photocopies of relevant sections of the handwritten minutes of proceedings of the Martel/Dixie Lee Baptist Church.

The summer 2003 issue of *Southern Quarterly* is a special issue devoted to the writings of Richard Marius, including the most recent published checklist of his works.

Nancy Grisham Anderson
Auburn University Montgomery
June 2005

Chronology

Richard Marius
29 July 1933–5 November 1999

29 July 1933	Richard Curry Marius, born in Martel, Tennessee, second son and third child of Henri Marius and Eunice Henck Marius
1948	Becomes writer for *Lenoir City News* and, in 1952, is promoted to news editor
1951	Graduates from Lenoir City High School; decides to enter the ministry during his senior year
1951–54	Attends University of Tennessee–Knoxville, living at home and hitchhiking to the university while working for the newspaper; reads "Man Against Darkness" by W. T. Stace for a freshman composition course
June 1954	Graduates from UTK *summa cum laude* with a degree in journalism

1954–55	Attends Baptist seminary in New Orleans, on weekends preaching at Baptist churches, primarily in Mississippi
1955–56	Attends Southern Baptist Seminary, Louisville, Kentucky
1956–57	Attends University of Strasbourg, France, on a Rotary Club scholarship studying Medieval and Renaissance history
1957–58	Returns to the Louisville seminary and receives B.D.
1958–62	Attends Yale University in the graduate program in religion, studying church history and Renaissance and Reformation history and writing a dissertation on Sir Thomas More; also begins serving as an editor of the Yale edition of More, work he continued into the 1990s; also serves as a pastor of the New Milford, Connecticut, Baptist church
	1959—M.A.
	1962—Ph.D.
1962–64	Becomes member of history faculty at Gettysburg College, Gettysburg, Pennsylvania
1964–78	Serves as history professor at University of Tennessee–Knoxville, becoming an activist against the Ku Klux Klan and the Vietnam War and for civil rights and freedom of speech (on and off campus)
1969	Publishes *The Coming of Rain*, his first novel, set in fictional Bourbonville, Tennessee, chosen 1969 Best First Novel by Friends of American Writers, alternate selection of the Book of the Month Club
1974	Publishes *Luther: A Biography*
1976	Publishes his second novel, *Bound for the Promised Land*
1978–98	Joins the faculty of Harvard University
	1978–94—director of expository writing
	1994–98—senior lecturer
1984	Publishes his first textbook on writing, *A Writer's Companion*

1984	Publishes *Thomas More: A Biography,* 1985 National Book Award finalist, alternate selection of the Book of the Month Club
1985	Publishes, with coauthor Harvey S. Weiner, *The McGraw-Hill College Handbook*
1985	Publishes *A Short Guide to Writing about History*
1986–96	Directs the Tennessee Governor's Academy for Teachers of Writing
1992	Publishes his third novel, *After the War*
1994	Edits and publishes *The Columbia Book of Civil War Poetry From Whitman to Walcott*
1996–98	Adapts *The Coming of Rain* into a play, which premieres as a repertory show at the Alabama Shakespeare Festival in 1998
1999	Publishes *Martin Luther: The Christian between God and Death*, second place, Catholic Press Association Book Awards
5 November 1999	Dies at home in Belmont, Massachusetts
2001	*An Affair of Honor*, fourth novel, released posthumously

[What Is a Preacher?]

In the second chapter of Acts, Peter appears as a preacher. He spoke to the masses on the day of Pentecost, and thousands were converted to the new faith. So I thought that I would take Peter as my chief example when I talked to you about the relationship of the preacher and his church, and especially about just what the preacher is. Peter is probably the best-known preacher in the New Testament.

Is the preacher supposed to be a god himself? I think that people demand this of the minister. In some way he is supposed to be more perfect than the people whom he attempts to lead. He is supposed to have mastered the business of Christian living so thoroughly that he is qualified to tell others how it is done. He is judged very severely for things that are accepted without question in the lives of other people. Some people will object if the minister smokes whereas they would never question this in someone else.

Perhaps delivered at New Milford Baptist Church, New Milford, Connecticut, 13 September 1959.

It is very fine for the minister to be a saint, just as it is all very fine for you to be a saint. And yet Peter was not a saint. I have great confidence in the New Testament record on this account. It would have been so easy to hide the weaknesses of Peter, but the people who wrote about him painted him as he was—a distinctly human individual. Peter thought about himself and power and glory. He would not admit that Christ could suffer, and Christ called him Satan after the experience of the Mount of Transfiguration. Peter denied Christ. You all know that story. It is often said that the experience of the Resurrection radically changed him, and it did. But it did not eliminate all his faults. In the fifteenth chapter of Acts, we have the description of Peter in the early Church. He was still buried in the Old Jewish law, unwilling to admit that God could love a hated Gentile so much as he loved a Jew. Peter was no saint—he was a terribly human being. And yet he was a preacher for God.

The preacher cannot be a perfect man. If you expect perfection from the minister, you expect the impossible, and you are going to be disappointed. The minister not only has faults—this is too minor a word—he has sin. He lives a sinner whose sins are not all in the past but whose sins are terribly evident in the present. Occasionally some minister is caught in some spectacular evil that makes the newspapers. People then have a chance to be shocked or horrified at this terrible example. But whether our sins are open or concealed, we are all sinners, whether we are ministers or not. In this we are the spiritual children of Peter.

Peter was a minister, but he had trouble with his faith. There is the story of his denial, the clearest example of this trait. I have said that everyone knows this story. But there are others. When Christ was taken in the Garden of Gethsemane, Peter cut off the ear of one of the soldiers. He was unable to have faith that Christ knew what was best. He could not understand that the Son of man had to suffer. We find him at other times in lack of faith. Thomas has come down to us as the unbelieving disciple. But much more is said of doubting Peter than of doubting Thomas. Peter was one of those in the boat that night on the Sea of Galilee when the storm came. He thought that Christ did not care if they died. Peter started to walk on the water and then sank.

Do you expect your minister to have perfect faith all the time? Some people do. Some people come to a minister expecting him to be able to answer all their questions. They expect him to have a direct line to God by which he can immediately know the will of God.

The minister is one like Peter who loves Christ. Peter faltered. He sinned. He had little faith. But he loved Christ, and he wanted to follow him. The minister is the one who shares life with his people. He shares their sins and their unbelief and their faltering, and he shares the forgiveness of his sins and the communion in Christ with them.

[Who Is Man?]

Who is man? In this question are the questions of religion. The reason man asks about God is to discover himself. Man—an animal? In many ways. He is a living creature with anatomical similarity to every other creature that has a backbone. He has a lifespan, cares for his children, suffers from diseases, fears things that animals fear, hides with them from fire in the forces.

But no man is exactly like an animal. To speak of treating man like an animal is repugnant. In our century we have seen this happen. We know what slavery is from seeing its grim resurrection in this the most civilized of centuries: Russian women herded by Germans like cattle to build tank traps; Jews in the concentration camps; the Cuban terror of Batista and the pouring out of blood in pits of mass graves in the aftermath of the new regime. To see man treated like an animal wounds something within the deep interior of the basic stuff that we are.

Perhaps delivered at New Milford Baptist Church, New Milford, Connecticut, late 1950s or early 1960s.

Why is a man different from a dog or an ape or any other animal? Man has the power to reckon with things that are not immediately visible. He has the power to remember concrete events, a power whose tool is the word—the sound that by common agreement is applied to the object. When I hear the word "dog," I do not usually think first of the letters "d-o-g," but rather I think of an animal that walks on four legs and chases cats. An ape knows to warm himself by a fire, but he cannot know to put another piece of wood on the fire to keep it from burning out. He cannot visualize that which he cannot immediately see.

But man is different. He can remember the past—and so we have history. He can meditate and reflect upon the present—and so we have conscious life. He can wonder about the future and what he has never seen—and so we have faith.

Man is the only living creature who can reflect on God. This is the meaning of the image of God. God and man are alike in that they are the only forms in the universe that can think about each other, even though man cannot see God. God can think of the sparrow's fall, but the sparrow cannot think of God.

Man can meditate on that which is to come. He can be afraid. I never saw a pig who was capable of worrying, even when he was being led to the slaughter house. He thinks only of food. A cat will sit down in a dark room and go to sleep. A man will sit there and dream about the past and the forgotten opportunity or the future and the cares that will be there. A man is different.

The clearest thing about the creation story in the book of Genesis is that man is yet the center of creation. It is here rather than any other place that modern science has made man afraid of what he is. During the Middle Ages, and indeed since the dawning age of mankind, man believed that he and his world were at the center of all creation. The Egyptians were characteristic of this belief. They thought that Egypt was the center of the world. On each side of the fertile Nile valley, the glaring sands of the desert stretched away to the horizons. They worshiped the sun. Each morning the sun, whose name was Amon or Re, rose in the East and marched across the sky, traveling carefully to look at his land. And when the day was done, the sun dropped over the western rim of the earth and sailed back to the East in the little boat, ready to arise again the following day. The Greeks said that the sun was a chariot, driven by the god Apollo across the sky each day. But no one doubted that the earth was the center of the cosmos.

And then Galileo came. And with his primitive telescope and by mathematical computation, he discovered that the sun did not revolve around the earth, but the earth revolved around the sun. The fear of the church at this point is understandable. They believed that man was the center of the universe, and if it were proven that the earth went around the sun, man would not be so important. But Galileo was not the last. After him came others, and now every school child knows more about the physical universe than the wisest of the Greek philosophers. We know that the earth is a minute body, one of a number of planets in a small solar system, a part of a universe that defies the imagination. At this point, how can the individual man be very important? It is easy for man to be saddened at the fear that his life does not mean anything. And if nobody cares for him, why should he care what he does?

The Christian faith, however, reaches down to this doubting man and affirms creation—that is, that God himself is interested in this man that He has personally made. This is not a biology treatise here. The point is not the method by which God brought man into being. The point is that it was not an accident, but it was a conscious work of God.

This also means that man has a destiny. Now a destiny is something other than an end. The destiny of an automobile is that it be driven along roads conveying people from place to place. It may end smashed against a tree with its passengers crushed to death inside. Man has a destiny given to him by God. This does not mean that every man or every woman who feels a call of God must enter the ministry or must go as a foreign missionary. It means rather that God has something for an individual to do in this world. The whole world was created by God—not just the part that relates to the world to come. God calls men and women to be school teachers and farmers and laborers and husbands and wives. If the work is honorable and of service to the fellow man, God can call a person to do it. Luther said that the kitchen maid who did her work in the house to the glory of God was a greater blessing than all of the monks who said their beads and sang their chants every day.

The point is: God has created the world, not merely the church.

So man is in the world. He finds it not as a prize which he has earned, but as a gift from God. Where do you come from? Have you ever wondered why you are in this place? By faith we live as if we receive life from God. We cannot prove this belief with sure and infallible reasoning. But we cannot prove the opposite. And we can live with the gratitude within us that this belief is so and that we have what we have because God cared for us.

Man is an amazing creature. This being the age of science and invention, it might be easy for us to assume man's infallibility. He can appear to us as a majestic creature. He might seem to be very nearly divine. We can assume a confidence in our power. But man is really not so great in himself. If you place a telescope on the sun, not one of the mighty works of man would be visible to the observer at that point. Recently I read of the deepest penetration of the ocean to date: some scientists went down four and one-half miles. But the earth is eight thousand miles through the center. Recently my cousin ascended in a balloon some eighty-one thousand feet into the outer reaches of the atmosphere. But who can measure space? Both in space and in time, man is a tiny creature. He comes onto the earth for such a little while. He has problems, he drops into scandal, he weeps for the lost roses of life, he loves, and he takes pride in his children and his work. And in a little while he is gone, and his work is gone, and all the problems which stirred through his breast are a part of the dust that remains. Today there is a strong feeling among scientists and writers and people who live to believe that man is an animal, and his life is meaningless. But the Christian faith proclaims to men in their limitations that God confers meaning on an otherwise meaningless existence.

[Christmas Eve]

> And so it was, that, while they
> were there, the days were accom-
> plished that she should be delivered.
> And she brought forth her first-
> born son, and wrapped him in swad-
> dling clothes, and laid him in a manger;
> because there was no room for them
> in the inn. (Luke 2:6–7)

This morning we meet in the joy of Christmas Eve. I think that
there is hardly a person here who has not been elevated by the joy
of this season. As I have said before, the reasons for this joy are
diverse. The joy itself depends on our own expectations about this
day and the fulfillment of those expectations. Also, as I have said
before, whether our joy is a true expression of our Christian faith

Delivered at New Milford Baptist Church, New Milford, Connecticut, early 1960s.

is sometimes difficult to know. Christmas is filled with so many other things besides our faith. To be able to know what this joy is in the context of the Christian faith requires a constant definition. It requires a constant examination of an old story and a continual retelling of that story which first the angels sang over the skies of Bethlehem a long time ago. That is the task of the Church, and that is the task of her ministers. It is a task which is easier to fulfill because of the elevation which this season brings and the certain openness of hearts who want to hear the story again.

But what is the story? It is more than a baby born in a manger. That occupies much of our devotion and time and concentration at Christmas. We think of Mary and Joseph and the baby in a straw-covered place, and off in the darkness we hear the gentle mooing of the cattle and the bleating of the sheep and the stamping of horses and the hard breathing of all the animals. This is Christmas the way it is shown on our Christmas cards, the way it is fixed in our minds. And we often do not see the rest. We often do not think that the manger smelled bad, that it was dark, and that Mary was probably afraid. As Martin Luther used to say, all the angels were out singing in the skies over the town, and not one of them thought to come to help Mary. She was alone. And she must have feared. The birth must have been hard for her, harder beyond all belief. I have often wondered what Mary would have thought if she could see the birth of Christ pictured in our Christmas cards. I think she might have asked, "What is that?"

Christmas is more than an isolated birth in a manger. It is more than the birth of a child and the coming of shepherds and the visitation of the wise men. It is more even than the star which appeared mysteriously in the sky and guided men to the manger-side. To say all this and to say nothing more is to fall short of the most important thing about this day. And that thing is that this child is Christ the Lord, that this baby born in humble estate and lowly poverty is the Word made flesh. And to understand what that means, we must go beyond Bethlehem. We must look beyond where the star shines, and we must listen to the secret Word of God behind the singing of the angels.

To understand Christmas, we must look at something which characterized the whole ministry of Christ on the earth. We must find that thing which caused the early church to burst with an enthusiasm that carried it over the known world. We must find that force which has preserved that church to this day through millions of unknown people who have had a part in carrying that faith to us.

That force, that power, that essence of the faith is that it is New. To look at the New Testament as a whole is always to be impressed with the New in the consciousness of the people in its pages. It is the New Testament, separate and distinct from the Old. The Gospel which Christ preached and lived in his person is the New. It is the New wine. It is the New cloth. It is the New commandment. It is the New doctrine. And Christ himself said that the cup was the cup of the New Testament in his blood. And finally he was laid in a New tomb. And after him, the Sadducees and the Pharisees accused the disciples of preaching a New doctrine, and Paul wrote, "If any man be in Christ, he is a new creature. The old things are passed away. Behold, all things are become new."

But what is the New? What is this essence of the faith? Most people would probably say that it is a New morality. Perhaps most Christians would say this. They would claim that Christ has come teaching people ethical rules which, when followed, will bring the Kingdom of God on earth. It is undoubted that Christ has brought a high ethical code. Sometime it is good for all of us to read the Sermon on the Mount recorded in the Gospel of Matthew. And it is good to take each verse and think about it in reference to ourselves. When we are told not to judge, we should think until we have found some situation in which we have been in a position to make judgment. When we are told to love our enemies, we should think of someone who is our enemy, and we should ask ourselves, do we love him? And so through the passage. Each verse should be a rule laid down by our conduct to measure it. After such a procedure, none of us can come off very well.

But moral conduct is not the characteristic of the Christian Church and its proclamation. There are other religions whose moral code is almost as high or just as high as that of the Christian faith. The Jewish faith demands ethical standards from its people. So does Islam, and so does Buddhism. So, in fact, do certain types of atheism. All of these things, and more, exhort their people to love one another, to do good, not to kill, not to steal, not to have disrespect for God. In all great religions there is a common concern for man and his life in the world, and there is a common striving against injustice, cruelty, and human shame. If we are Christians merely because of the ethical standards of our faith, we have placed our faith as one among many others. We have robbed it of its distinction. And without that distinction, we find the faith itself robbed of that very force which makes it what it is—its uniqueness.

The New in the Christian Gospel must always be brought back to the person of Christ himself—this one whose birth we celebrate at this time. The New is his whole life, his death, and his resurrection. All of the life of Christ is what we celebrate at Christmas because that life began there. And what is that life? That life itself is the New. And because of its newness, it is powerful. Because that whole life was something new, the joy of Christmas has endured across nearly two thousand years. It has passed from nation to nation, from language to language, from persons to others, and it is preserved for us today. It is a joy which will last after we are gone, and our faith is such that we believe that it will last to the end of the world.

To understand just how new the life of Christ is in the world, we must try to understand what this world is without Christ. That is not difficult. For today most of the world lives as if Christ did not exist. And we can look at the world simply as men imagine it to be.

Without Christ, we encounter a world that seems to turn in a meaningless cycle. Things seem to go round and round without any point, without any goal, and without any end. All the world, all of life seems to be on a wheel turning in empty space, and the people upon it are reduced to prisoners without hope.

We encounter the cycle of life every day. The day itself is its most constant example. The sun rises in the morning to drive the darkness from the world, and the day comes to earth. The hours pass, the sun marches across the sky, and in the evening darkness steals in from the East and gradually fills up the earth again. Primitive man feared the darkness much more than we do now. When it came flooding into his valleys and covering his hills, the world was filled with danger and a shiver of fear. And wild beasts stalked out of the range of his firelight, and dogs cried off in the deep woods. And life continued—the cycle of the welcome sun and the fearsome darkness.

There is the cycle of the years. Spring comes to the world, and the green things come out, and the crops begin to grow, and people begin to breathe afresh the air of life. To me one of the most beautiful sights in the world is to look at a ridge dark through the winter with somber pines and cedars and in the spring to see that ridge begin to burst with the light green of other trees. But after spring comes the summer, and after the summer the autumn, and then the hard north wind drives the dead leaves from the trees, and the air is cold, and our lives are spent looking out of windows into a dead world. Christmas itself comes on the day after the solstice when the day begins to grow again. Always the turning, always the cycle—nothing is permanent.

So it is with human life. There is the growing season of the spring days when children come with wide-eyed amazement into the world and look around them into life. There is the summer of work, of toil, of growing into maturity, and, hopefully, there is the autumn of reward, of harvest of all the labors which men have done. But always there is winter, the long and hard days of old age, and the end of our earthly pilgrimage. No matter who we are, we cannot escape this cycle unless our lives are cut off before they are completed.

And as it is with the individual human life, so it is with the life of man in general. He builds his nations from the decaying refuse of old civilizations. And from that garbage dump of the old, something new arises. Soldiers go out to fight on distant frontiers for their nation. Statesmen give their lives formulating policies that will make the nation strong. The citizens of the nation live in a glow of idealism when they consider their place in the sun. Men have worked hard, and what they have erected may seem for a time to be permanent. But it is not. Every nation which has ever arisen on the face of the earth has fallen away in time. Nothing is permanent. And we have no assurance at all that the things that we have done in this nation will last to the end of the world. That is the way of the world. In all of man's existence, there is a wheel turning, and in time, it carries all our work away.

I think the nature of this cycle in human events is characterized by the New Year festival which we shall celebrate next week. We shall welcome the New Year as an innocent child, and we shall wave away the old year in the person of a tottering old man who wanders off to oblivion. And all over the world people shout in an enthusiasm of joy because the old is gone and the new is come. All the mistakes of the old have been wiped away, and a new page of life lies before us. And with the new, we have hope that we can write something better, something more pure. We find ourselves in the mood of Tennyson's poem:

> Ring out, wild bells, to the wild sky,
>> The flying cloud, the frosty light:
>> The year is dying in the night;
> Ring out, wild bells, and let him die.

> Ring out the old, ring in the new,
>> Ring, happy bells, across the snow:
>> The year is going, let him go;
> Ring out the false, ring in the true.

But at the end of every year, we have the same shouting and the same songs to sing. The new year has become old, and it is stained, soiled, and torn just as all the years of the past. The wheel turns, and we are drawn upon it.

What does this mean to us? It means that something of immense value has gone out of our lives. Man was created in the image of God. That does not mean that he was in form like God because God is a spirit, and man is body and spirit. But it means that man has in a small measure certain attributes that God has to perfection. Of these, perhaps the most important and most all-inclusive is the power to create. Men crave to create something, to do something that will bring something new and valuable into the world. All men have this. The very demand of our society that men pile up things is a warped notion of creation. When we stand before a pile of possessions, we are deceived into thinking that we have created something. The frustration and the emptiness which possession alone brings are symptoms of something else—the frustration of man's desire to create something. The artist or the poet or the thinker in some other discipline works from an inner impulse to create something. But this is not the sole possession of those people we ordinarily call "creative." It is a characteristic of every man. And every man achieves his true nature in so far as he is able to create something, whether it be a loving family, a job well done, or an attitude of soul which receives the world.

But to see life as it is lived on the turning wheel is to be in despair about all our creation. Creation is a difficult process. It takes work, toil. Creation does not come to people because they may be born in a certain place. It is something which pulls at the inner fiber of our being. And it is a life-consuming process. But to live in a world without God is to know certainly that everything we create will someday be carried away. All that for which we labor, all that for which we sacrifice, all that for which we spend the bleeding moments of life, will be taken away in time and will pass into oblivion. Somehow the weight of that passing of things presses upon us. And unless we can fill our minds with activities, with petty worries, with our routine, with the little things which plague us, we feel depressed. How difficult it is in American society to be alone! How difficult it is to take long, solitary walks! For we do not like to be alone. And I think that the reason we do not like to be alone is that we do not like to face ourselves and our lives. When we are forced to think of our dreams and how they are shattered, we are depressed. When we are forced to ask ourselves, what does this life mean, we feel a certain gloom come across us. Yet we must ask ourselves these questions. That is a part of humanity, of our being men and not pigs. We must ask what this job means. We must ask what our family means. We must ask what our goals in life mean.

And outside the person of Christ, I am convinced that all these questions end in a negative answer. For the world, looked on in itself, is a world that is deprived of hope. It is a world drawn out on the wheel, and the men who live in this world are prisoners to a turning destiny over which they have little control.

This is the root of our hope in Christ. For to believe in Christ is to believe that God himself has come into this world where we live. This is why the historical proclamation of the Church is so important: Christ is God and Man in the world. Neither of the two sides of the nature of Christ taken alone is sufficient to our needs. If Christ is only man, then God has not come to us, and Christ was subjected to the same cycle that encloses mankind. If Christ is only God, then God has not shared human life. This does not explain how God is in Christ, but it affirms that he is. And that is why Christmas is New. This is the coming of the all-powerful God into human existence. This is the breaking of the old cycle of things, for it is God who has taken the wheel upon himself and shattered it with his coming. God has come from outside man's life, to take that life upon himself, and by that act to raise to himself all men who believe.

So the man in Christ does not stand upon the wheel. His existence is not a meaningless cycle which neither he nor any other mind can comprehend. But that existence becomes taken up by God. For God has come to him and taken that existence upon himself. And from that act, no human being in Christ can ever believe again that his life has no point. No one who is in Christ can believe that the things which he tries to create in God will pass away. For the man in Christ believes that all his striving, all his suffering, all his loneliness, are taken up into the eternal mind of God where it is not forgotten. Thus, the man in Christ can face life every day. He can do what he is called on to do whether it is little or big, and he can live in the assurance that he will not be judged by its failure, and he will not be held accountable for its success. He is able to face each moment in the knowledge that this particular moment has a meaning in God's heart. He will be able to walk in the limited light that we have in the world because he has faith that God's eyes see beyond his own human power to comprehend. Then the apparent cycle of life is set on another level. He sees the turning. He sees how things pass away. He sees how his own life is going. But these things do not make him despair. For he sees a deeper reality behind the reality of things seen. He lives in the assurance of things not seen, the evidence of things hoped for, and that is the life of faith. It is a life of triumph—triumph not at the head of armies or before cheering multitudes or in the blackened pages of history books. It is the triumph of little things, the triumph of cleaning the house and raising the family and helping the neighbor and living in the life of faith put upon us day to day. It is the triumph of belief that this life, as we have it, is a trust from God, to be lived to his glory and in the gratitude of his grace.

And this is the New in history at Christmas. This is the New in our lives. This is Noel, the birth of something which is new and green in our hearts—the birth of hope and the promise of peace. And it began at the first Christmas, now a long time ago, when Christ came to dwell among men. It began with the angels singing and the wise men coming and the baby sleeping in his manger bed. It began in ways which defy the reason of men, and it has continued in ways through time to now which continue to defy man's mental powers to lay hold of the event. That baby, poor and weak and born in poverty, has broken the powers of darkness and brought light into the world.

As the French carol says, "For four thousand years the prophets have promised us this. For four thousand years we have waited for this happy time. He is born, the holy child."

What Do We Do with Jesus?

But if he will not hear thee, then
take with thee one or two more, that
in the mouth of two or three witnesses
every word may be established.

And if he shall neglect to hear
them tell it unto the church: but if
he neglect to hear the church, let him
be unto thee as an heathen man and
a publican.

Verily I say unto you, Whatsoever ye shall bind on earth shall be
bound in heaven: and whatsoever ye

Delivered at Tennessee Valley Unitarian Church, Knoxville, 26 February 1978.

shall loose on earth shall be loosed
in heaven.

Again I say unto you, That if
two of you shall agree on earth as
touching any thing that they shall
ask, it shall be done for them of my
Father which is in heaven. (Matthew
18:16–19)

What do we do with Jesus? This subject is something that I have
always been interested in because there is a way in which, in East
Tennessee especially, you simply cannot get away from Jesus.
Now you find him thrust at you all over the place. He arises
at times in the classroom. Only a few weeks ago I had what
amounted to a kind of testimony in one of my classes, and my
response at that time, as always, is to say, "Well, thank you very
much. I'm sure we all appreciate this," and go on. I recall years
ago when I was lecturing to the freshmen in Western Civilization
a boy came up to me and grabbed me by the arm and said, "Dr.
Marius, have you been saved?" I simply looked at him and said,
"Well, I'll be damned!"

Well, I guess that the burden of my remarks today is simply to
say that Jesus and I have had a very, very long relationship together
and that it has been disappointing on both sides. I think when I
was a kid that I expected Jesus to stand around and make sure
that life was always comfortable, that I always had a sense of
meaning and purpose, and that I always knew what I was doing
because Jesus would tell me what I was doing and obviously if I
were doing what Jesus wanted me to do, I must at least have some
idea of why I was doing these things—I hope you can follow that.
On the other hand, it didn't work out that way, and I have found
myself disappointed in Jesus for being used for just about any
sideshow that comes down the track, and seemingly being able to
be adapted to everything from Billy Graham to Anita Bryant without any qualms whatsoever.

I think Jesus has been disappointed in me for not being
more reverent toward him and not being more considerate of

his problems. There have been many, many times when I have felt that perhaps the worst thing that has ever happened to East Tennessee, and perhaps to the country at large, has been Jesus because Jesus has allowed people to have a benign mask to hide wickedness behind, and I think that we have always seen that. Nevertheless, you can't get out of it quite that easily. In some sense, the Western tradition is stuck with Jesus; in some sense, the Unitarian Church is stuck with him. He arises with us from time to time and must be considered because of the nature of the culture that we have and the nature of the people that we are. I think that it is a very interesting thing to see just how many ways the Western tradition has tried to use Jesus, and what I see in all of this is a collection of needs that are met in different ways in our history. One of the things I suppose that all of us could probably agree on without too much trouble is that fundamentally we have a fluctuating mystery whenever we come to talk about Jesus.

I think it is a very useful thing for us to read the Gospels. I think it's a very useful thing to read the Bible and to know what is there. One of the things that happens to us when we do read the Gospels is that we become aware of a man of whom certain things are said that we simply cannot now believe. However, we might also go on and say that the Gospels probably do not tell us much about what the real Jesus was like.

One of the things that the Campus Crusade for Christ people I meet at the university are always saying is something that one of their gurus of the present, a man named [Francis A.] Schaeffer, who always styles himself as "Dr. Schaeffer" so some people will know that he is educated, has written in a book called *How Should We Then Live?* [*The Rise and Decline of Western Thought and Culture*]. The book was given to me by one of my students over Christmas, and I actually did read a few chapters in it. One of the points that he makes, that is made by these people, is always this: if Christ is not who he said he was, then he is either a madman or a charlatan, and the assumption seems to be, since we all know Christ is a good man, that we must then believe that he was exactly who he was. Well, the fact is we really do not know from the Gospels exactly what Jesus said about himself. We do not know the details of his life. We see a shadow floating behind the Gospels that we can never truly grasp.

And yet I think it is really an interesting thing to see how many ways people in different ages have made a lunge at the shadow. I suppose, probably, most of us in this room have at some time or another stood in one of the hundreds of Gothic churches and cathedrals and had to contemplate that still and awesome Christ who presides over the last judgment; sending some people down into some stone monster with its jaws open, representing Hell, and others being elevated to the skies by the angels under Christ's command. And that figure itself is so stern and so still it indicates in some way that reality, and religious reality especially, is not something to be taken lightly. It has always been interesting to me that the chief characteristic of the Middle Ages is always disorder. It was an extraordinarily harsh and disorderly and awful time. It was a period when, as Thomas Hobbes said in contemplating life without a state, "Life was solitary, poor, nasty, brutish, and short," for great numbers of people, and yet the desire of the age was always for order. The desire was for stillness. The scholars read Aristotle, and Aristotle's God is fundamentally a still God, a God who rests in a kind of eternal calm. And the ideal of the Middle Ages that is found reflected again and again and again in so much of medieval literature is to penetrate the screen of disorder that surrounds us and to get back to something that is orderly. Every time I see that Gothic Christ standing in that judgment in the cathedrals and see that stillness and see that soberness, I think that here is the longing of the age for something that will stand still and something that will not move. In some real sense the Christ that the Middle Ages came up with was a Christ in direct contradiction to life, but in harmony with the idea that so many people possessed.

When we get to the Reformation, we find Luther saying that God is always activity, activity, activity. God is always doing things. God is never still. And you have resurrected in Luther, I think, this God of the Old Testament and New Testament alike—

I think especially the Old Testament—who is always doing things, is never predictable, is here and there and always acting in such a way that people can recognize here is God. But they could not ever say exactly why God is doing this or why God is doing that. I think that really is Luther's God. And the Reformation is very hostile to pictures of Jesus, and Jesus does not arise as something in Reformation art that one perceives by means of statuary or by means of painting. It is very seldom that you have people in the Reformation stressing any sort of picture of Jesus. One reason, of course, was that people in the Reformation felt that this was idolatry and to have any picture of Jesus was to begin to worship that picture instead of the invisible God. But I think probably another reason was that this Jesus of the Reformation is summed up always in motion, always moving, always doing, in the same way that God is always in motion, always moving, always doing. And, therefore, this God could not be captured in some sort of picture that would be eternally still. This is a different age, an age when people are in motion in Europe, an age when society has many, many barbarities to it, many horrors to it. And fundamentally people, as a result of many things happening, are beginning to see a kind of stability in towns and in countryside alike that leads to a glorification of the active person and so, consequently, you have a glorification of the active God which you find in so much Reformation art, and you can't capture that active God in a still picture.

It is an interesting thing that once again when you come into the nineteenth and twentieth centuries you find a whole lot of pictures of Jesus, and we all sort of know what they are. We have them thrust at us on billboards. We have them thrust at us in the movies, and it's always, at least until *Jesus Christ Superstar* and a few things like that, that Jesus was always poor and simple. Jesus was always calm. He was always peaceful, in many ways like the medieval Jesus. And there is a curious thing about him. He always seems to be very, very poor, and he always seems to be especially prized by people in the upper-middle class. It is an interesting thing how we sometimes take our religion and make images of a religion that we, ourselves, in no way intend to follow. The people who go to the Christmas pageant that is presented at the Coliseum every year—which, alas, I have never seen—drive away in very, very large automobiles, dressed very, very nicely. The children are dressed very well to see this thing, and none of these people, to my knowledge, ever said, "I am going to look at this poor baby Jesus lying in straw in a manger where cows and calves and goats and sheep are and give up all of my wealth, sell my car, and become poor myself."

There's a curious way very often in which we in this age, and people in all ages, who are religious make other people and images of an idea which we in no way intend to follow, but because we pause and give some reverence to the ideal, we tell ourselves that we, too, for a moment are poor. We, too, for a moment are simple. We, too, for a moment are not simply lost in this jungle of the possessions which make so much of our lives. We make other people live up to the ideal, or we make an image live up to the ideal, and we go our way without any thought whatsoever that we ourselves will live up to this ideal. The liberal Jesus that was produced sometime in the nineteenth century—this Jesus, sweet and mild—this Jesus who is a real sweetie, a real darling—this Jesus was preached in the upper-middle-class churches.

It is very interesting sometimes—kind of sickening, but very interesting—to go back and read some of the sermons of a New York minister, Phillips Brooks, who was called around 1900 a prince of the pulpit. When he died, life in New York simply stopped, and all sorts of dignitaries came to his funeral, and he was eulogized and solemnized and entombized, I guess, with tremendous glory. Well, if you read his sermons, what you find always is the ideal propounded of the good of wealth. I remember one particular sermon where he talks about the way a person of any sort of discrimination can recognize the truly wealthy man without any trouble by that man's conservative dress, by his dignified walk, by the way that he nods his head, and by the way that he is generous to his children. One can also recognize the person who is a fraud, who is trying to look rich but really isn't rich, because you can see in the kind of clothes *that* person wears, and the kind of way *he* strides along the street and the kind of way *he* greets people with a kind of obsequious quality that you do not find in the real rich. So, says Phillips Brooks, you can tell the *true* Christian from the person who is only pretending to be a Christian. It's an interesting metaphor because it just demonstrates the way that this Jesus sweet and mild that Phillips Brooks talked about all the time was really the Jesus who was somehow the sort of ideal for this wealthy middle class of America's gilded age.

I think as Unitarians—I think this is one of the reasons why I became a Unitarian—that we all sense the way in which Jesus should be treated as if he is dangerous. Because there is a tremendous way in which any religion stressing monotheism, stressing a full revelation in one person, is always likely to bear with that stress a lot of very, very bad things. I think I may have shared with you once before something that I read in the American poet Karl Shapiro, who, of course, is a Jew, who had a little essay in the *New York Times* some years ago about what he felt as a Jew around Easter time and how he felt in Gothic cathedrals. He said he could never forget the time when he went into a Gothic cathedral and saw the art and could never forget that so frequently the preacher in the cathedral would extol the resurrection of Jesus on Easter morning and then at the same time damn the Jews who had killed Jesus and send the Christians on Easter afternoon into the Jewish ghettos to loot and to burn or to kill people in honor of this Jesus who had arisen that morning. He said it really did give him a lot of pause to see the revival of interest in Gothic.

Now I think that all of us can probably, as I have just indicated, find ways in which there is something really dangerous about so much stress on Jesus in so much of our history. Every time I read any article on the new evangelicalism, which the national news magazines always seem to praise, I think to myself that the new evangelicalism is likely to bring with it a new intolerance. And I wonder what people who do sincerely feel themselves born again, saved from death, saved from the curse of plenitude most of us live with all the time can feel after a while toward those of us who do not have that Jesus, do not believe in that Jesus, do not want that Jesus, and do not want the culture that is associated with that Jesus. There is always something a little frightening to me about the thought of one-fourth of the American religious public now going to the evangelical churches and now believing so passionately in this particular Jesus, carrying along with them all the baggage that sort of belief is likely to include, even sometimes when they do not really understand what they are doing. It is most frightening because it is an intolerance that does not really recognize itself. It provokes rather the sort of wonder that I have already described: "You mean you don't believe in Jesus?" And their absolute incredulity that people are capable of living lives that are somewhat rewarding and somewhat happy without this sort of Jesus. I think that always when we come to talk about Jesus we should have with us this sense of the dangerous that is there.

And yet it does strike me again and again as I grow older and look around that one can reject a lot and yet at the same time one may still retain something. I am a little bit disturbed—not a lot disturbed—by the way in which the world now seems sunk in a kind of hopelessness about what we are and who we can be. I just got through reading a book by Wilfred Cheek called *Transatlantic Blues*, which is a kind of autobiographical novel of a man who feels himself lost in the world and confesses to a tape recorder. The book begins by this man trying to give his confession to somebody in the first-class compartment of an airplane. The result is that the man to whom confession is being made assumes that the confessor is mad, so he takes refuge in a Sony tape recorder and that really is the novel. Well, the man who is talking is supposed to be a kind of Johnny Carson character, a television person who interviews people and has an international following and has no roots. I must say spending several hours with that book gives you a kind of feeling of the utter hopelessness of the lives of a great many people—the utter lack of reward, the utter lack of any sort of personal relationship, and the sense that this is the way life inevitably is. I hope I am not simply reading a pessimism of ten years ago into a culture of today, but it does strike me with great force that we are living in a world where many people who are helping to form the culture have in some sense given up on the possibilities of human existence. Therefore, we have passed into a kind of exploration of our own experience to the detriment of the social concern that human beings should have. And we examine this experience completely apart from any idea that there is in it some hope or some possibilities to be anything other than what Cheek depicts it as being in *Transatlantic Blues*.

It does seem to me that human beings are always caught in the nutcracker. On the one hand, I have just been rejecting those people who believe that they have found all the possibilities of human existence in Jesus and believe that the believing evangelical Christian is the only person who knows how to live and that this person not only knows how to live but possesses abundantly all the possibilities of life including a tremendous amount of steady joy. I have a cousin who used to be a missionary who went to South America to save the Catholics from the Pope several years ago—he was a very nice person—and I just yesterday morning happened upon a batch of letters that I had received from him about fifteen years ago. They inevitably conclude, "with full joy and peace in our blessed saviour, Jesus, yours, Bob." I was reading these letters, and I thought, "Well, I guess that's why Bob and I never really got along together." There was a way in which he always rushed on me with the idea that "I have it all in Jesus and life is perfect because I have it all in Jesus." Well, we want to avoid any sort of making an absolute of any idea we profess, or any cause that we espouse, any thing that we are. There is always a way in which human beings should stand under judgment, should stand under the judgment of not having achieved what we know in our minds probably is the ideal.

And, yet, on the other hand, it seems to me that human beings must avoid falling into utter despair, and it seems to me that we must never allow ourselves to live the sort of religious life or social life where we say, "Nothing really matters. Nothing makes a difference. Life is just one vast sewer." Well, I had a friend one time—twenty years ago we were at the University of Strasbourg together. He was from Canada, and I was from Tennessee, and we were talking about life, and he said, "All I want to do is float upward in this vast cesspool full of frogs that life is, and get to the surface and take one deep clear breath before I die." He became a university administrator! And I don't know whether he is still swimming upward or not. Well, it does seem to me that this sort of cynical attitude of despair is one that human beings just cannot accept if society is to go on. And I, personally, have a great desire to see society go on.

Well, I do see the image of Jesus, willy-nilly—perhaps not the image I would have chosen had I been God making the world. I do see the image of Jesus as something that we can perhaps use in both ways. It certainly is true, and cannot be denied, that Jesus has been used for horrible things in our past, but it is also true that people have been able to use Jesus also as a judge *against* the horrible things. I think that all of us can see that there is a Jesus who does speak to the Jesus that is willing to burn people and the Jesus that is willing to persecute people and the Jesus that is willing to be arrogant and proud. There is a Jesus that judges the Jesus some people possess and that says, "You don't really have the person you claim to have or the person you think you have." Yet there is this other Jesus that does affirm that something is possible in our lives. There is a Jesus, in other words, that keeps us from walking between the two poles—of presumption on the one hand and despair on the other. And I am beginning to say that—perhaps in our lives, perhaps in our culture, perhaps in our art—we might as well take this Jesus and use him to good account, because I think that there is here something that is worth using as a means to communicate to the world out there, something we need to study, something we need to think about, something at times we perhaps even need to preach as Unitarians, something that is worth using to keep human beings from either bowing their necks to despair or stiffening their necks in arrogance.

The God beyond God

I am surprised to see myself here this morning. When the invitation came to speak at this service, I thought that I should accept it because it would be a way of learning something about Harvard. Earlier this week I came several times to see what was going on, and so for the first time in a decade I found myself at Christian worship. Once I heard someone very near my nose uttering the Lord's Prayer; I discovered to my astonishment that it was I.

I was brought up in a home where my mother read the Bible aloud to her children every day. I was destined by her to be the preacher in the family. So I attended two divinity schools and got a degree from one of them and then found myself happily sitting at home on Sunday mornings listening to Beethoven. My Christian faith slipped away like water spilled out on the ground that cannot be gathered up again.

The loss of faith begins very early for most of us, and we do not really have to go to divinity school to accomplish it. Even yet

Delivered at Morning Prayers, Appleton Chapel, Memorial Church, Harvard University, 31 October 1978.

I think often of something that happened when I was no more than fourteen, growing up on a farm in East Tennessee. Once at night after church I fought in the woods with a new boy in the way that old boys will. His father was a renter, a sharecropper. He was taller than I was, and I was a little afraid of him. But when I hit him, he fell like a bale of straw, and I learned for the first time that children of owners are usually heavier than the children of renters. A little later he went hunting, and he banged the stock of an old twelve-gauge shotgun against the ground, and the gun went off into his stomach, and he died on a very cold Thanksgiving Day.

The boys in his Sunday School class were his pall bearers. He was buried at a place called Shady Grove far out in the primitive country where his people were from. Still I remember how heavy he was in death as we struggled from the black hearse up the rocky little knoll in a forest clearing where the graveyard was.

When I was old enough to drive, I went back to Shady Grove alone one night for some vague and adolescent purpose. I stood in the graveyard and heard the wind moving in the dark, and I knew in the sure way we know some things that none of those people would rise again and that no trumpet of the Lord would fill the skies with wings and light. And I am not here this morning because I have changed my mind.

Yet we are all here to share in an ancient ritual, and I expect to come again. As I grow older, I find that the familiar rituals of life are dearer than once I thought they were. They are curious in that we say in them some things we do not quite believe so that we may affirm other things that we believe profoundly.

What can we believe about ourselves? Are we only the descendants of killer apes endowed with a corrupt genetic inheritance that dooms us fatally to bloodiness? Or is it possible that we are made for each other and that the natural state of human life is a community we must embrace before we can be truly ourselves?

Martin Luther said that every Christian is *simul justus et peccator*, just and sinful at once, and his insight is true in a mythic way even in a world where God is still. We are not merely one thing or the other; we bear about ourselves always, as Johan Huizinga said of the Middle Ages, the smell of blood and roses, anarchy and community, violence and love. In one way or another, all our rituals are expressions of the inexorable yearning of human beings to hold each other dear.

As Luther saw, the yearnings of the just are never in this world fulfilled. Civilization is never so good and the community never so perfect that we may be at ease in Zion. But in Luther's view the struggle is never lost either. While we are sinners, we are also just. And we never quite sink to a state of depravity that really allows every man to make war against every other man so that the life of all becomes, in Thomas Hobbes's phrase, "solitary, poor, nasty, brutish, and short." Something is always working to pull us back from the edge of that pit. And that something lives in our common rituals.

St. Anselm said that God is that, greater than which nothing can be conceived. It is a remarkable definition. He did not say that God was the greatest thing we can imagine. He meant rather that once we define God, we must admit that our definition cannot begin to comprise the thing it strives to grasp. I don't think that a St. Anselm matured in the autumn of the twentieth century would be shocked at my remarks this morning. To him God would be yet more than the God in whom we cannot believe. The God beyond all our definitions cannot be contained in dogmas or data. We put out hands to each other and find him. We say old words and sing familiar songs together, and we uncover the mystery of the common life affirming itself yet again and winning one of those small victories that keeps civilization alive.

[Hope and Tribulation]

Not long ago, on my morning bicycle commute from Belmont, I topped a low hill and smelled wood smoke drifting across a snowy landscape. It brought back in a powerful, Proustian way a Saturday morning in my adolescence when I was hunting rabbits in one of our infrequent snows in rural East Tennessee. I came across a rounded hill and smelled wood smoke from the nearby farmhouse of Mr. and Mrs. Cedric Nance. My boots were wet, my feet were cold, and my fingers were numb from gripping the Winchester .22 rifle in my thinly gloved hands, and the Nances had four daughters.

The thought of fried rabbit suddenly lost much of its appeal, and I ended by sitting away the morning by the big iron stove in their kitchen, the air filled with laughter and stories and the smell of the fire, and decades later on a snowy day in Cambridge the unexpected fragrance of wood smoke suddenly brought back that lost moment.

Delivered at Morning Prayers, Appleton Chapel, Memorial Church, Harvard University, 13 February 1984.

The Nances were fairly typical of families in our neighborhood. Perhaps they were poorer; they did not have electricity. I loved to sit at night with them and hear stories under the magical glow of kerosene lamps. Like most families they had a cistern and had to carry water inside, and they had an outhouse instead of a toilet. They washed their clothes in a black iron pot over an open fire in the back yard. Mrs. Nance was huge and jolly; Mr. Nance was as thin as a tomato stake and had a tubercular cough. The Nances were all deeply religious, but that was not noticeable in the country where everybody was deeply religious—even the people who refused to come to the Midway Baptist Church because they said it was filled with hypocrites.

My ninety-year-old father and my two brothers still live on the place where I was born and grew up, and I go home frequently to see them.

The neighborhood has changed. Knoxville, which John Gunther once called the ugliest city in America, has crawled almost to our doorstep in a cancerous blight of shopping malls, car dealerships, asphalt parking lots, flashing lights, and suburbs where all the houses look alike and everybody has a two-car garage. The Nance house is gone. So is the home of the spinster sisters we called the Grable girls—three women in their eighties who lived in a rambling old white house in the isolated Hardin Valley. They had an icy spring that gushed up out of rocks, and in the hot, slow summers I used to walk over there sometimes to visit and to get thirsty and to assuage my thirst with that wonderful water. A few years ago Interstate 40 crashed down through the Hardin Valley on its way to Nashville and swept the house of the Grable Girls away (they were long dead anyway). The spring became polluted by septic tanks from new homes built on the ridge above, and it was walled in and its waters diverted into a huge concrete storm drain that no one would think to drink from.

The people have changed as much as the land itself. The story-telling tradition has been swept away by television as completely as the house of the Grable girls by Interstate 40. In the subdivisions that have grown up around our farm, people live closer together but know each other less. Years ago when the meanest woman in our neighborhood fell over dead in her garden, the preacher came to our house to tell my father that he had to be a pallbearer. My father didn't want to be a pallbearer; nobody wanted to be a pallbearer for that woman. I think the only reason we went to her funeral was to assure ourselves that she was really dead. But the preacher said nobody could die in our neighborhood without the proper forms, and so my father and several other conscripts dutifully carried her corpse to the grave. Today I suspect she could fall over dead and not be noticed until the buzzards began to pick her bones.

I can ask some gloomy questions about all this. Is this all that the New Deal and TVA and the labor unions have wrought? Did the political and social reformers who worked so hard to save our region accomplish nothing but the destruction of a community? No. The answer is no. For a lot of other things are gone from our neighborhood, too.

Segregation is gone. Tuberculosis is gone; diphtheria is gone; bad teeth in adolescents are nearly gone; the outhouses are gone; the cisterns and typhoid fever are gone; illiteracy is gone. A friend—high school drop-out and son of a dirt farmer—boasted to my brother recently that he was $100,000 in debt for his tractor-trailer rig. With that rig and others, he has put three children through college.

The most endangered religious virtue nowadays is hope. Hope is the anticipation of change for the better, and at first glance, much change seems for the worse. I wish change in our neighborhood had been more selective. But although Christian theology demands hope, it reports original sin—which means that the best of our hopes crash out of control once they are set in motion towards reality and bring some results that we did not anticipate or desire. I sense that many old-time liberals feel deeply disappointed at what their political and social activism has wrought. Many have sunk into nostalgia and narcissism and apathy. We do not like even to think of tomorrow and tomorrow and tomorrow, much less devote ourselves to making them other than sound and fury.

But religious people are required by their profession to hope and to persevere. Things will never work out exactly right. To the Christians at Rome Paul wrote of hope and tribulation almost in the same breath, urging joy in the one and patience in the other. It is not a bad message to this age.

[Light]

> And the earth was without form
> and void, and darkness was upon the
> face of the deep. And the Spirit of God
> moved upon the face of the deep.
> And God said, let there be light;
> and there was light.
> And God saw the light, that it
> was good. (Genesis 1:2–4)

The daily almanac in this morning's [Boston] *Globe* tells us that we will have ten hours and forty-five minutes of daylight today. On December 21, we had nine hours and four minutes of day. The sun is moving north, the days getting longer. In little more than a month the days will be longer than the nights.

Delivered at Morning Prayers, Appleton Chapel, Memorial Church, Harvard University, 19 February 1985.

I have been at Harvard seven years now, but I have not yet grown accustomed to the early winter darkness—lights glowing in the Yard sometimes by 3:45 in the afternoon, the sun sinking lower and lower to the South as if some unexpected wobble in the rotation of the earth might fling us into perpetual night, Cambridge and its world sunk in Milton's "darkness visible." Then in late December the light begins to come back, and at this time of year we may glance out of a window onto a frozen world and realize suddenly that it is past 5:00 and still bright, and our hearts somehow leap higher than the thermometer.

Harvard is, of course, an advanced place. But living here makes me feel close to the primitive thing dwelling within us all. Sometimes as I bike back and forth between here and Belmont through those darknesses from November to now, I hear what Raymond Carver has called "the rumble of the centuries," the distant cry of our anonymous ancestors before the fear of winter and the creeping night, their joy at that moment—about December 25—when they could see the victory of the sun over the dark, the night in grudging retreat before the swelling days.

Our faith pulsates with the imagery of light in conflict with the dark. At the beginning of Genesis we read that darkness was on the face of the deep. "And God said, Let there be light, and there was light." This was a miraculous light indeed since only later in the Creation story does God create the sun, the moon, and the stars. The authors of Genesis did not make a foolish mistake; they believed that God Himself was the source of light, and they wanted no sun to assume some independent divinity. God spoke, and creation glowed. The Psalmist spoke to God "who coverest thyself with light as with a garment," and expressing his trust in God, he said, "If I say, Surely the darkness shall cover me, even the night shall be bright around me."

These grand metaphors of divine light have the familiarity of clichés. I mean no pun when I say that they deserve continual reflection by the religious. I am increasingly dismayed by the savagery of so much religious expression throughout the world. Of course this savagery is hardly new. A couple of weeks ago on a rainy London morning, I stood alone in the quiet of the Assyrian

Basement in the British Museum, caught up in the drama of a low relief mural carved in stone and depicting the triumph of Ashurbanipal over the Elamite king Teuman in the Battle of the River Ulai almost three millennia ago. The stone river is gorged with the arrow-pierced dead of Elam. Teuman and his eldest son, Tammaritu, lost their heads to Assyrian swordsmen. The details are exquisite. To hold a body still during a decapitation, an Assyrian soldier stands on the hand of the fallen warrior whose head is about to become a trophy. Naturally the Assyrian gods bless the carnage and receive the gratitude of Ashurbanipal for it.

The benevolence we associate with religion has been a near thing. The history of our own faith leaves us precious little room for middle-class condescension towards the Assyrians. Hitler's soldiers wore belt-buckles with the inscription "Gott Mit Uns" stamped on them, and I have heard a recording of the prayer an army chaplain prayed for the crew of the bomber *Enola Gay* just before it flew to Hiroshima with an atom bomb in its belly. I need hardly recite for this assembly the horrors being done in the name of our religion and others around the world right now.

Yet our own faith keeps affirming against much evidence—evidence found within the bosom of that faith itself—that God is good. And that assertion, so perplexing and sometimes seemingly so meaningless, displays a mysterious might that does condemn the atrocities committed in religion's name.

I wonder if the original notion that God is benevolent arose in that primitive time when someone by a great leap of the imagination conceived and believed that God and light are one. If nature is God's mirror, we see in it only with difficulty a benevolent face. I grew up among farmers, and as a child, I had no trouble believing that the same God who created the king snake to crawl into a robin's muddy nest to devour the young despite the shrieking of the bird kingdom in our yard could also cast those into hell who failed to serve him with enough zeal. And an innumerable multitude this morning stands ready to die for its various faiths and ready to kill for them, too.

And yet God is light, and whoever first saw the identity of God and light started us along the way to some sort of check on our natural impulse to make God the servant of our worst conceptions of him. Indeed the metaphor of light helps us see that there are a better and a worse to our notions of divinity and to our conceptions of our own nature.

In this time of year, we have one of those paradoxes of human experience. Winter is still with us. More snow will fall; more ice will form in the streets; more sand and slush and salt will pour together in the ankle-deep marshlands that streets become in the Cambridge winter. But every day the sun rises a little earlier and sets a little later and stands a little higher in the sky at noon.

There are seasons of life, and one of the most dangerous of human fallacies is the belief that some revelation will bring us to eternal summer. In this world we will never get beyond the revolving of light and dark. We live in a society seemingly ever more cynical, ever more convinced that good is only a social convention, and that since all social conventions are relative, there is no worthwhile difference between what we once called good and once called evil.

On this day when we have ten hours and forty-five minutes of daylight it is worth remembering that the very notion of God as light is a benevolence, a judgment on any part of religion or life that is not kindness.

[Lourdes]

I biked into Lourdes one hot day this summer. My wife and our fourteen-year-old son swept down a narrow mountain road out of the Pyrenees, and there was the town where in February 1858 a fourteen-year-old girl named Bernadette Soubirous saw a vision of a woman in white in a grotto near the swift river Pau. In August of 1858 a stone mason who had lost the sight of one eye and was about to lose the other made a compress of mud from some of the earth where Bernadette had seen her vision. He regained his sight.

Since that time several million pilgrims have come to Lourdes seeking a vision of God. Many have been sick unto death, coming to Lourdes in one final burst of despair and hope. Nothing else works; why not try the Virgin Mary? Now and then someone reports a miracle of healing.

In 1963 on a similar trip I stopped off in Lourdes and attended a 6:00 a.m. mass at the grotto. It was cold and drizzly. Around me

Delivered at Morning Prayers, Appleton Chapel, Memorial Church, Harvard University, 24 September 1985.

hundreds and hundreds of sick people in two-wheeled covered carts pulled usually by family members gathered for the service. The sick were of all sorts and of all ages. I remember particularly a young man in his twenties, wearing an expensive white sweater, his skin pale as marble and his lips, a brilliant and unnatural scarlet, his thin hands folded patiently on the blanket over his lap while an older man—I supposed his father—pulled his cart as close as possible to the altar set up where Bernadette had seen the strange apparition long ago.

Nearby the river roared down out of the mountains with a melancholy sound of cold. I leaned against my bicycle which I had pushed into the sacred enclosure and heard the silence of that waiting multitude, faint hearts lifting up to the last chance. And I imagined some red-neck healing evangelist out of my rural Tennessee childhood standing up front and yelling at all those people that if they would only have faith, they would all be cured of everything from corns to cancer and hop right out of those carts and go off shouting glory hallelujah, stopping of course by the collection plates on their way to the exits. I recall standing there in that colorless light of 6:00 a.m. with my arms folded, and with the soft rain pelting down, and preparing to mock the priest in my heart. But the priest began his prayer by saying, "Dieu notre père, nous vous prions pour ceux qui aujourd'hui vont mourir" ("God our father, we pray to you for those who today are going to die"). It was easy enough to see that many of those people huddled there in the rain were going to die that day or another day soon. It was not a prayer that lent itself to mockery.

On this sunny day in July we arrived at the enclosure on a Saturday afternoon while thousands of healthy men and women and children from just about everywhere were parading around in the processional of what was called a day pilgrimage. Their faces were everything from deep contemplation to a certain stiff composure of the sort that I have seen people wear when they attended concerts of music they did not understand. We did not enter the enclosure and go to the grotto. We were all three in shorts, and signs in many languages asked people in shorts to stay away.

We watched for a while from the outside, caught up in contemplation almost in spite of ourselves. Then we left. At a bridge just beyond the sacred area, we made a wrong turn and paused for a moment to study our Michelin map. I was standing there, my legs straddling the crossbar of my bicycle, the map spread out on the handlebars in the brilliant sunshine, when a family walked silently by, pulling one of those carts in the direction of the sanctuary. In the cart was boy about the age of my own sturdy child waiting ahead of me on his bike. This child was thin and sick, his skin the color of a sliced apple that has been exposed too long to the air. As his family pulled him by, they every one looked at my son, and the sick child in the cart turned his head so that his eyes held my own boy for a moment. My son, who in nine years has never missed a day of school on account of illness, looked suddenly down at this slowly passing child with a start of surprise. Nothing was said. But I thought, somewhat incongruously perhaps for a Catholic shrine, of young Siddhartha the Buddha riding through the sunny park and coming on the sick man, the aged man, and the corpse.

Later, peddling on through the green mountains behind my son, I reflected on the desperate patience that brings one to Lourdes. On that earlier trip years ago I said in curious exasperation to someone there, "Qu'est-ce qu'on fait ici, si on est malade" ("What does one do here if one is sick")? "On attend" ("One waits"), he said.

So far as I know we have no curative shrines to the Virgin Mary here in the United States. Waiting is not an American virtue, and our religion—whatever it may be—does not much value the still small voice. Jerry Falwell and Jesse Jackson and most preachers in between preach sermons designed to set the multitudes in motion. At times it seems that any religion that touches the American people becomes afflicted almost instantly with the symptoms of nervous disorder or at least with a certain comfort in the hyperkinetic.

My sentiments are with Jesse Jackson and Dan Berrigan and with many another who wants to move human society towards justice. I see few reasons ever to wait in the effort to relieve the injustice inflicted on the neighbor.

Yet individually we all encounter that inevitable part of life that Lourdes represents when we are ground against helplessness, contradiction, frustration, and the temptation to despair. We must abide with time and sickness and death. At some moment, if our religion is to teach us truly and if we are to meet our human condition with honesty and honor and courage, we must learn to be still and alone in those rooms of the heart where no one can enter to be with us, where the questions are not answerable, and where we can only wait.

[Martin Luther King Jr.]

And then cometh Jesus with them
unto a place called Gethsemane, and
saith unto the disciples, Sit ye here,
while I go and pray yonder.

And he took with him Peter and
the two sons of Zebedee, and began to
be sorrowful and very heavy.

Then saith he unto them, My soul
is exceeding sorrowful, even unto death:
tarry ye here, and watch with me.

And he went a little farther, and
fell on his face, and prayed, saying O
my Father, if it be possible, let this
cup pass from me: nevertheless not as
I will, but as thou wilt.

Delivered at Morning Prayers, Appleton Chapel, Memorial Church, Harvard
University, 18 January 1987.

And he cometh unto the disciples,
and findeth them asleep, and saith
unto Peter, What, could ye not watch
with me one hour?

Watch and pray, that ye enter
not into temptation: the spirit indeed
is willing, but the flesh is weak.

He went away again the second
time, and prayed, saying, O my Father,
if this cup may not pass away from me,
except I drink it, thy will be done.

And he came and found them
asleep again: for their eyes were heavy.

And he left them, and went away
again, and prayed the third time, saying the same words.

Then cometh he to his disciples,
and saith unto them, Sleep on now, and
take your rest: behold, the hour is at
hand, and the Son of man is betrayed
into the hands of sinners.

Rise, let us be going: behold, he is
at hand that doth betray me. (Matthew
26:36–46)

Last week I watched the first episode in the PBS series on the Civil Rights movement. I sat in the semi-dark before a television screen and felt a prodigious wash of memory. A very young Martin Luther King Jr. in Montgomery in 1955 spoke in those cadences that became so familiar to so many of us before he was gunned down by a murderer only thirteen years afterward. And a dark world of hatred, violence, and evil did not melt but did retreat before the dream that King and others lifted in the night.

What touched me more than anything else was an interview with Dr. King during the turbulent Bus Boycott. Was he afraid? No, he was not afraid for himself, he said carefully after a short pause. What he was doing was more important than a single life, he said. Fear could not stand in the way.

I suspect that Dr. King *was* afraid. But his cause ruled his emotions.

Dr. King was the best speaker I have ever heard. We remember the extraordinary passion of his magnificent voice. But it was always the passion of reasoned judgment. He said this: Americans claim to be apostles of freedom; most Americans make religious professions. If these things are true, it follows that blacks must be released from bondage because black and white together we are citizens of the same country and worshipers of the same God. The message was as logical as Euclidian geometry, and that logic fueled the passion that was as a consuming fire.

Some of us have lived through a lot of passionate nuttiness. I recall a night in 1970 just before the killings at Kent State when I got a call at eleven o'clock from the Chancellor's Office at the University of Tennessee. A band of radical students had occupied the Student Union building. They claimed they had "liberated" the building. No one knew why. But someone suggested that I might be able to talk the students out of the building before the police moved in. My caller told me that I would have until 1:00 a.m.

I ran to the building and was allowed to enter. I had some credit with the students. I had made the first speech in Tennessee against the Vietnam War and had spoken all over the state for the peace movement. With three others I sued the university in 1968 when our chancellor refused to let Dick Gregory speak on campus; William Kunstler was our lawyer; we won, and Dick Gregory came. So many people called me to tell me they were going to kill me that for a long time I slept with a loaded revolver on the floor next to my bed. So the students let me in, and there followed a long debate between me and their leaders over the wisdom of this particular move.

It's not important here this morning to repeat that debate. I could not tell them that the police were gathering outside to storm the building. That would have created in them a compulsion to prove that they were brave enough to withstand the police. That, in turn, might have got somebody killed or maimed for life. The Knoxville police had applauded and cheered the news of Dr.

King's murder. I had to debate the students on their terms, much of the time standing on a table while perhaps two hundred of them pressed around me.

It was a mad scene. Many of the students had painted their faces with red and purple dyes. Their leader, a blond, white young man, was wearing what looked like a mattress cover, though later I was told that it was an African tribal robe. There was a great deal of yelling. But at 12:40 a.m., they left the building, shouting defiantly—but leaving.

I walked back home and crossed Cumberland Avenue, the main street that went through the university area, and, down the hill in the darkness under the huge trees, I saw motion and detoured to investigate. Dozens of black-uniformed police in riot gear lounged about carrying long clubs, and black prisoner vans were lined up and waiting for the assault that now would not come, and suddenly I realized how close this thing had been.

I despised the Knoxville police, but I was fiercely irritated by those students who had provoked a meaningless confrontation. Dr. King's confrontations, though fueled by passion, were always engineered by rational purpose.

Many people in the 1960s went about urging us to "let it all hang out." It meant that we should do whatever we felt like doing at the moment.

I have always believed that it is better to keep most of it tucked in.

The Gospel stories imply that if Jesus had followed his rawest feelings he would have fled the cross, and if he had followed the passions of the mob, he would have revolted against Rome. From what we know of Dr. King's short life, it seems clear that he lived with anxiety and that if he had followed his most primal feelings he too might have fled his cross or worse, let his rhetoric collapse into virulent vehemence.

Very often, if we are to be moral people, we must assert our will over our most powerful emotions and make ourselves do those things that reason tells us are right, though our emotions may tell us to run away or to make some passionate gesture merely because we feel like doing it. But not much of anything worthwhile comes out of undisciplined raw emotion. Dr. King left us a rich legacy of social passion. He also left us a legacy of disciplined and rational moral action that has endured and will prevail.

[Martin Luther King Jr.]

Finding God
in Strange Places

> And Jacob awaked out of his
> sleep, and he said, Surely the Lord
> is in this place; and I knew it not.
> (Genesis 28:16)

My mother read the Bible to us every day when I was growing up, and this was one of my favorite stories. I must confess that I also love the sentimental hymns that have sprung from it—"Nearer My God to Thee," "We Are Climbing Jacob's Ladder"—I hesitate in naming some like these lest my dear cousins Kathryn [Nichols, former minister of music at this church] and Mark [Brombaugh] disown me for my musical vulgarity.

Noel Coward somewhere has a line about the power of bad music. Such music evokes memories. One of mine is of my

Delivered at the dedication of the organ at First Presbyterian Church of Lansdowne, Philadelphia, 1 March 1987.

mother's somewhat stern taste in church music. At the Midway Baptist Church where I grew up, we sang our Sunday morning and Sunday night hymns from the old Broadman Hymnal. But on Saturday night we had what we called singing conventions. Mother refused to attend these gatherings. I loved them. We had solo singers, duets, trios, quartets, quintets, and sextets. If we had more than six, they were usually something like the Spears Family or the Cleavelant Derricks or something like that. They intended to sing in close harmony, and they did most of the time. They were often accompanied by a pianist who, if he or she was any good, was said to "tear that piano up."

I guess gospel music is akin to the blues—it is repetitive and has a heavy beat. The subjects are almost always hardship, death, and the mansions waiting on high. Despite their recognition of sorrow, they exude detailed hope, often lovingly describing the furniture of heaven. Sometimes the braggadocio of the songs is a trifle suspect:

> Here on earth you may talk and brag about
> > All your wealth untold
> > About your silver and your gold.
>
> Mansions on display, homes in bright array
> > Mock me as I roam.
> > But wait till you see me in my new home.
>
> If a mansion you're sporting,
> > while the devil you're courting,
> > wait till you see me in my new home. . . .

Sometimes singers were accompanied by guitars, and sometimes by trombones. I loved the tenors who seemed to trill off the ceiling on some of the high notes, and I loved the bass singers who could go so low that you thought you were going to have to drop a rope off the lower end of the piano to pull them back up to daylight. I always used to wonder why bass singers were skinny and tenor singers were fat; and I still don't know the answer to this perplexing question.

The books they sang out of had shape notes, as we called them; most of them were published by the Stamps-Baxter Music

Company, and all of them had thin paper backs. Mother despised Stamps-Baxter singing as she despised guitars and trombones in church. I think she worried when people enjoyed their singing too much or when the rhythms made young people think about dancing. No good hymn could come out of a limber-backed hymnal. That was one of her undying convictions. She trusted the good old Broadman Hymnal because it had hard covers. When Billy Graham came along, she loved hearing him on the radio, but she worried a little about his limber music. Before she died she worried about all the limber songs that were getting into hardbound books.

In 1981 I attended the Southern Baptist Convention in Los Angeles to write a story about fundamentalism for *Esquire* magazine. I was startled to discover that fundamentalists have now developed rock-and-roll choirs with singers in purple polyester tuxedos who hold microphones in their hands and dance all over the stage belting out their lyrics while the choirs throb behind them. Mother had been dead nearly ten years by then. But I could almost feel her disapproving spirit at all this cavorting.

As I have indicated, I reveled in the gospel music that Mother hated, and to tell the truth I still enjoy it. But I have come to appreciate Mother's feelings. The problem of sentimental hymns is that they tame the mystery of God too easily and make affirmations that are too—well, too sentimental, as if life will be good if we can be made to feel good. They promise too much; they make faith too easy. That is the great weakness of fundamentalism—the notion that no matter how bad life is, certainty about faith and nearness to God make everything wonderful. The sentimental hymns make it seem as if God were a great, friendly dog, ready to come leaping into the room whenever we whistle for him.

Fundamentalists in my day loved the testimony meeting. People stood up in church, often weeping, and testified about all the wonderful things God had done for them, all the wonderful answers to prayer, all the great conversion experiences, relief from great burdens, the last words of the dying, and so on. These people claimed to be certain that God had spoken to them as directly as a human friend might speak. His message was always something they wanted to hear.

My wife is a Unitarian and a devoted one. She is patient enough to endure a great deal of good-natured kidding from me when we come together for Sunday dinner after our son and I come home from our church and she comes home from hers. "How many people were saved today?" I'll say. "How many verses of the invitational hymn did you all sing before somebody came down to the altar?" Now and then I go to church with her, and somehow I was not surprised to discover that the Belmont Unitarians have instituted a testimony meeting. People happily get up and tell all the good things that have happened to them lately and why life is worth living. They convey the notion that if you just count your blessings and think good thoughts, everything turns out all right.

And I have observed that the general optimism of the fundamentalists and the optimism of the Unitarians are very much alike. They just use different language to express it. Not long ago [17 November 1985] I was asked to speak in the Belmont Unitarian Church [the First Church in Belmont Unitarian–Universalist] at the Sunday morning worship service. I spoke on "Why I am not a Unitarian." [According to that morning's order of worship: "Missing Mystery: A Problem of Liberal Religion"; no copy of that presentation is available.] I said that I loved the Unitarians and their relentless energy and their implacable demand that everybody do social good. But I mentioned my reservations about Unitarian optimism.

I told the story of my old Lutheran department chairman at the University of Tennessee who some years after retirement died of leukemia. I went to see him in the hospital a couple of days before the end. He was lying on his side, and I sat next to his bed and held his hand. "Dr. Hoffman," I said, "you've meant a lot to me and to lots of other people. Your life has meant something." He gripped my hand strongly and wept softly. Suddenly I was aware of his Unitarian daughter leaning over him and gesturing frantically, jerking both of her thumbs up. She was making motions with her mouth. I got up and walked around the bed and said to her, "What?"

"Be upbeat," she whispered furiously. "Don't talk about dying."

The fact that her father *was* dying and seemed to want to talk about it didn't matter. *She* didn't want to talk about it. So very many times I have heard fundamentalist preachers in the South stand over a corpse and declaim, "Our brother is not dead," and behind them the electric organ croons some sentimental hymn that nobody in the room can believe just because it is so sentimental. That's the real curse of fundamentalism and of Unitarianism, I guess: they inject huge infusions of sentimentalism into their faith in hope that the right kind of feeling can still the doubt and brighten the dark. Most American religious expression tends in that direction; so I should not appear to single out one or two groups. We tend towards sentimentality in our religion. But sentimentalism never quite sees the human experience as we know it across the sweep of life.

Jacob did not feel sentimental at Beth-el. I suppose we can make a fairly good psychological case out of Jacob. He had cheated his brother Esau out of their father Isaac's blessing. Esau was angry enough to kill Jacob. Rebekah, their mother, wanted to get her favorite son away from danger. So she and Jacob concocted a scheme to get Isaac to permit Jacob to leave. Isaac was the patriarch, the law-giver for the family. Nothing could be done without his permission. Rebekah convinced him that Jacob should not marry any of the neighborhood women. He had to go back to her own land, to Haran where her brother Laban lived, and fulfill a mother's dream—that her son marry a woman just like her.

So Jacob set out, apparently alone and on foot. The book of Genesis says that at sundown he took stones and put them around him for pillows and lay down to sleep. It was a nameless place. "A certain place," the Bible says. An ordinary place, probably lonely and remote and hidden, perhaps prey to wild animals roaming at night. Then he dreamed and saw the ladder reaching up to heaven and the angels of God ascending and descending, and God himself stood above the ladder. The Bible does not say that Jacob *saw* God; to see God was to die. But Jacob knew God was there, standing above the angels, the messengers of God ascending and descending, and God spoke and made Jacob the great promise:

I am the Lord God of Abraham thy father, and the God of Isaac; the land whereon thou liest to thee will I give it, and to thy seed:

And thy seed shall be as the dust of the earth, and thou shalt spread abroad to the west, and to the east, and to the north, and to the south; and in thee and in thy seed shall all the families of the earth be blessed.

And behold, I am with thee, and will keep thee in all places whither thou goest, and will bring thee again into this land; for I will not leave thee until I have done that which I have spoken to thee of. (Genesis 28:13–15)

Jacob waked up then. And he uttered these words, "Surely the Lord is in this place; and I knew it not." We should take his sentiment literally. Jacob apparently shared a common belief in his region, that his God was limited to his soil. There were other gods; but they, too, were limited to their own particular lands. Years later, Naaman the Syrian came into Israel to seek and to find a cure for leprosy from the prophet Elisha. And when he was cured, he stood before Elisha and said, "Behold now, I know that there is no God in all the earth, but in Israel." Naaman had to return to Syria to serve his master. But he said to Elisha, "Shall there not then, I pray thee, be given to thy servant two mules burden of earth? for thy servant will henceforth offer neither burnt offering nor sacrifice unto other gods, but unto the Lord." Why did Naaman want to take two mule loads of earth from Israel back to Syria? The Bible doesn't tell us. But the general agreement of scholars is that Naaman thought the God of Israel could be worshiped only on soil that came from the land of Israel. Even the Lord God Jehovah at that time seemed bound in the minds of some worshipers to His own land and His own place.

So our best estimate of Jacob's situation is that here, at Beth-el, in the middle of the night, alone, away from kith and kin and all he knew of life, he awoke from his dream, his vision, and realized suddenly that although he had crossed the border away from his father's lands, his father's God was still with him. He found God in an unexpected place.

Jacob was on his way to learning for us something of the mystery of monotheism. Religion is a lot easier when you believe in many gods. With many gods, you can shape different gods to different experiences. My sixteen-year-old son and I have spent a lot of evenings this year reading *The Odyssey*. Odysseus resembled Jacob in so very many ways—crafty, a wanderer away from home, always in danger, always barely surviving, but surviving nevertheless. Everything seems so simple in *The Odyssey*. His patron god is Athena. But Athena is not all-powerful, and when Odysseus offends the god Poseidon, blue-haired god of the sea, Poseidon goes to war against him, and Odysseus cannot get home. Athena and Poseidon argue their cases before Zeus. The travail of a man becomes cause for disputation among gods.

But Jacob was on his way to the discovery that there was only one God. And that presents terrible problems. In a monotheistic universe, that one God has to be found everywhere. That God must be in every experience. We cannot flee Him; we cannot escape Him. "Surely the Lord is in this place," Jacob said, "and I knew it not." And somehow God has to be in all that we see as good and all that we see as evil.

This is not an idea that on reflection lends itself to sentimentality. Jacob must have waked up from his dream in the middle of the night with the darkness all around him and the stars wheeling overhead. He had seen the angels, and he had heard the voice of God, and that voice had made him a great promise. Out of Jacob would come a mighty nation. Jacob was not to be an isolated speck coming into being and vanishing then without a trace; Jacob was to have a history. He was to be remembered as long as earth should last.

One might imagine after God spoke to him that Jacob might have burst forth into a stanza or two of "We Are Climbing Jacob's Ladder." Or he might have sung under special inspiration a few verses of "Nearer My God to Thee." He might have at least laughed and clapped his hands and danced in the dark. God had spoken to him; obviously on his waking Jacob still felt that tremendous presence. Surely everything was now going to be beautiful.

But Jacob had no such thought. The Bible says, "And he was afraid and said, how dreadful is this place! This is none other but the house of God, and this is the gate of heaven." God spoke to Jacob and Jacob was terrified. Again and again the presence of God does that in the Bible; it terrifies even those who worship Him. God's holiness seems ready to dissolve humankind, human understanding, human values.

When the morning came, Jacob got some control over himself, and he did some of the conventional things that people do to reduce the terror of God and to bring religion under control. He built a temple; he did some bargaining; and he made some promises.

> And Jacob rose up early in the morning, and took the stone that he had put for his pillows, and set it up for a pillar, and poured oil upon the top of it.
>
> And he called the name of that place Beth-el. . . .
>
> And Jacob vowed a vow, saying, If God will be with me and will keep me in this way that I go, and will give me bread to eat and raiment to put on,
>
> So that I come again to my father's house in peace; then shall the Lord be my God:
>
> And this stone, which I have set for a pillar, shall be God's house: and of all that thou shalt give me I will surely give the tenth unto thee. (Genesis 28:18–22)

In the middle of a dark and lonely night Jacob saw a terrifying vision of God. But in the reassuring light of day he undertook to reduce that vision to something he could handle in daily life. God had appeared to Jacob when Jacob was asleep, totally passive, not expecting anything of the kind. It was all God's doing. Jacob simply received. But now Jacob started making a contract with obligations on both sides. If God would do this and this and this, Jacob would do some things for God. Jacob asserted his control over the religious situation. He made God what Jacob thought God ought to be—a person in need of human promises and human devotion, so much in need of the tenth that Jacob promised Him that He would give Jacob the desires of Jacob's heart to get it.

All this sets religion on a nicely rational basis. We do something for God; God does something for us. We make God predictable by doing the right things. All this makes God tame, familiar, manageable. There's a sort of Catch-22 involved. We make God less terrifying by setting up some sort of conventions by which we bargain with Him on the assumption that He needs something that we can give Him, that is, our devotion. "If you will give me those things, God, I will worship you." And then something goes wrong, and we blame ourselves. Everything is so rational; and if that is so, we are at fault.

We can all tell stories of people we have known who in the face of irrational disaster sought to blame themselves because that was the only way they could impose meaning on their experience. It seems like a terrible and self-destructive practice. Victims blame themselves. It happens so often that we must infer that people would rather blame themselves than admit that there is no reason for things that happened.

Put together enough things that happen, and we have history. Jacob was an individual, and God promised him a history that would be a blessing to the nations. That is essentially all God promised him. He did not promise that it would be a happy history or a good history. He simply promised that Jacob would have a history that would extend for a long, long time.

We have our own history, and we are here this morning to commemorate the history of this congregation and to pause for a moment to recognize a triumph—a new organ. We can think of the joy, the consolation, the meditation the organ will now create here and in the history that is to come. That is the obvious thought. But we can also think of the money the organ cost and perhaps the debt that will now have to be paid off. I suspect that along with today's services there may come some appeals to dig down into your bank accounts or to push up against your credit-card credit line and produce some more cash to pay off the organ.

That common obligation of financial support is an affirmation as important as the music the organ will create. It indicates that you believe in one another, that you accept your community in this moment in history, and that your past offers some promise that you will have a future together, that you are willing to sacrifice something in the present for the sake of the decades to come. I don't take such things lightly.

It would be tempting at this moment to summon up all the good things in the history of this congregation and to make it seem that from its founding a century ago until now everything has run on in an unbroken stream of progress. The temptation of all such moments as this is to make history inspirational. Then I could point out all the great accomplishments of the church, all the times that it had triumphed over evil, how it had risen above hardship, endured, prevailed, walked gloriously all the steps along its way to this morning.

But I am unable to follow such a course for two reasons. The less important is that I do not know the history of your congregation. I know Stan [Reverend Dr. Stanley Niebruegge]. I know that my dear cousins have served here. I came down to Kathryn's ordination two years ago and sat on the front row with her, holding her hand while Mark thundered at the old organ you then had and a row of robed and somewhat forbidding looking ministers lined up against this forward wall here and prepared to quiz her on her faith. I wanted to say to her, "Are you sure you want to go through with this?" But I was moved by that ceremony and that celebration, moved by your demonstrating community and love and mutual responsibility. So I am here today in some trepidation to speak on this lovely occasion. But I don't know the history of the First Presbyterian Church of Lansdowne.

Stan might have sent me a book or a pamphlet, and I might have informed myself. I suspect that such a work would have delivered the sort of history that I have mentioned. This congregation has always stood for the right things. God has always been at home here. When we have come to the First Presbyterian Church through the years, we have always expected to find God here. Indeed it would be an insult were I to say suddenly and in an awakening tone, "Surely the Lord is in this place, and I knew it not."

But the main reason that I have not fallen into that sort of history is that I believe it is too easy, too sentimental, too likely to create unbelief even as we are declaring that we believe in it.

If we believe in one God, we must believe that He is in history. And yet that is one of the most difficult of all beliefs because history itself can be so terrible. The feminist writer Adrienne Rich has written, "We can't have a history if we want only to hear the tales of our best moments, our finest hours."

I suppose it used to be fairly easy to follow the track of God through history. You had to be fairly comfortable yourself, member of the so-called dominant culture that had done all right, and not know about the suffering of others. Or if you knew about that suffering, you had to put it off somewhere, make it an abstraction, pretend that it happened only to people you read about in the newspapers who would be displaced by other people you read about in the newspapers on the next day, people you could learn about over your morning coffee and your eggs and toast. American Indians, blacks, Hispanics, women working in sweatshops, children working in coalmines, might have written American history, for example, in a somewhat different way from what we read in our high school textbooks. But they didn't have the chance to write that history, and so it hardly existed. Those who did write history could say that God was on their side.

But in the video age, suffering presses in on us more closely. And it becomes harder to deny. It is possible to deny it, but more difficult than it once was. Like you, I have seen the TV evangelists. Like the Brady Bunch or the Waltons or a thousand other TV shows that have come and gone, the evangelists have learned how to make everything come out right in an hour, including the commercials. In that neat and ordered time-frame, everything becomes neat and orderly, and all the suffering of the world can be thrust away by waving a Bible and shouting at it and promising to pray for those who send in a donation.

But then there is a program like the recently concluded and magnificent *Eyes on the Prize,* a documentary on the Civil Rights movement, and we see again some things history is—Alabama state troopers clubbing and tear gassing non-violent marchers in Selma in 1965—and we see present-day interviews with some of those white Alabamians responsible for that violence, and twenty-two years afterwards they are unapologetic and seemingly proud of what they did to be brutal and to stand in the way of justice. We have movies like *Platoon* to show us Vietnam, but more moving perhaps are the photographs and the memories of My Lai. And we have the abundant documentation of the Holocaust. That sort of presence reduces the vapid sentimentality of Jerry Falwell to the level of Disney World, where people certainly enjoy the illusions but know that they are illusions and that when they leave the gates, the real world with all its terrible mystery is still there, still looming overhead, still threatening.

In this sort of world even Jacob's utterance seems almost too much. "Surely the Lord is in this place, and I knew it not."

Yet that is the hope of our faith. I think it becomes almost sacrilegious or blasphemous to convert that hope into some argument that pretends to demonstrate just how God was present at this or that terrible moment in history. I know that there is an almost invincible impulse to find meaning by making such arguments: white racist southerners murdered blacks and whites, men and women to prevent Civil Rights from coming to blacks, but in the end justice triumphed, and those martyrs were vindicated. That kind of talk can be inspirational, but it doesn't come easily to me. I keep thinking of the men and women who died, and the families who lost them. It goes only so far. How do we say of the Holocaust, "Surely the Lord is in this place, and I knew it not"? How do we say of cancer, "Surely the Lord is in this place, and I knew it not"? The moment we try to understand in detail and to explain, we begin to trivialize tragedy and to rob history of its truth. I was always irritated by those fundamentalists in the South who were so quick to explain disaster by saying to a grieving family that had lost a child to some violent death, "God must have a purpose in it." In the calamities of life I want to find purpose: I want to find God there. But I don't want some sugar-voiced person who has not suffered that calamity to tell me easily that God is there. Yes, it is a paradox.

We can approach history or our own experience with a dogged affirmation that God is there. But we cannot see God there any more than Jacob could see God in his vision. We see only the messengers of God in faith ascending and descending, joining creation to the creator, messengers who give some form, some vision to religious faith without explaining it in ways that reason can comprehend.

That does mean something. It means that we accept history and the society that history creates as a place to live and work. It means that we do not cease our journey in frustration because we cannot understand it all. Jacob went on his way after Beth-el and lived his life and died in Egypt and was embalmed at the command of his son Joseph and his body was returned to his own land of Canaan. He knew glory and sorrow. But he died with the glory *not* fully revealed and with his people in a foreign land that would become a land of bondage. Only centuries later did those writers who put the scriptures of Israel together find a pattern in his life that he surely could not himself see. From Jacob's own point of view, his life must have represented an almost epic chaos.

And that is our fate too within history. We do not know what it means; we trust that God is in it; and we must live on and work in that trust without ever expecting that all will always be well. We must find some individual purpose of our own in the evil. I cannot see or explain or even very well believe that there could be any purpose in the Holocaust. I cannot tell you what your suffering means. But I can look at the horror and find a purpose for myself in standing against any national impulse that might bring the horror back again. I can find a personal meaning in my calamities. I can find a personal meaning in the calamities of others, though I cannot tell others what meaning they should find.

But history is not all horror. We do have the glorious moments, the glimmerings of revelation. This Sunday morning represents a glorious binding of our past and our future, our statement of faith that we do represent a community that endures and that has a purpose, our confession that somehow we have been gathered out of all time and in this little space called earth to be one together. I cannot tell you what the history of this congregation should mean to you. You must hear God's voice speaking through that history to you, and you must decide then what purpose you take from it.

Our moments of glory are surrounded by the night when a stone serves as our pillow and darkness and loneliness and terror abound. If we will define ourselves as religious people, we are required to say that somehow God is there, too, in the darkness and in the terror, requiring some response from us. In the darkest night, we can dream a dream for ourselves at this moment, in this place, and for the future.

True faith always exists over against unbelief. The religious person says, "I believe," knowing that that very affirmation recognizes a contrary affirmation, "I do not believe." Faith looking at history with integrity must recognize the temptation not to believe. But faith responds with a dogged affirmation. And at the most dreadful moments in history, we must say with Jacob, "Surely the Lord is in this place, and I knew it not." And we take our own purpose from that affirmation, and journey through Jacob's terror-filled night towards the bright morning.

Christian affirmation rests on three virtues, faith, hope, and charity. Faith tells us what we affirm. Hope looks to the unseen future when we trust that our faith will be vindicated. And charity makes us bear one another's burdens until the day comes, and the night dissolves in the dawn.

Saul and the Witch

Scripture: I Samuel 28–31.

The story of Saul and the witch of En-dor always frightened me when my mother read it to me in my childhood, and as an adult I can see why. Saul, Israel's first and doomed king, sees the gathering of the Philistines to subjugate Israel. The Philistines have come in from the sea—always a source of mystery and horror for Israel—and they know the secret of iron and fight with iron swords. There is not a blacksmith in all Israel, and Saul knows that the very existence of his people is at stake.

The god who has made him king will not speak to him, whether "by dreams, nor by Urim, or by prophets." Since no one among the living can console him, Saul turns to the dead, to Samuel the prophet who had anointed Saul and then cursed him and died. Saul's men locate a witch at En-dor, and disguising himself, Saul goes to her at night to ask her to call Samuel from the grave.

Delivered at Morning Prayers, Appleton Chapel, Memorial Church, Harvard University, [1988?]. Published in *Best Sermons* 1. Ed. James W. Cox (New York: Harper & Row, 1988), 84–87.

So Samuel's ghost comes up from the earth at this midnight summons, but he pronounced not hope but doom. "You were not bloody enough," the ghost says in effect. Saul had not sacrificed Agag, king of the Amalekites, before Yahweh and, for that offense, says the ghost, "Yahweh will let your people Israel fall into the hands of the Philistines, and, what is more, tomorrow you and your sons will be with me."

So it was. Saul was terrified at Samuel's bloody prophecy, but he was no coward. This was the Saul who had come home one evening from his plowing only to learn that Nahash the Ammonite had besieged Jabesh-Gilead and had offered to lift the siege only if he might gouge out the right eye of every man in the town. Saul, stirred by fury and pity, rallied Israel and fell on the Ammonites and massacred them until, the Bible says, "no two men were left together."

But then came the Philistines, and even Saul's courage could not triumph against iron swords. "Tomorrow, you and your sons will be with me," Samuel's ghost said. The next day, Saul's three sons—Jonathan, Abinadab, and Malchishua—were cut down by the Philistines on Mount Gilboa, and Saul, "wounded in the belly by the archers," as the Bible says, told his armor-bearer, "Draw your sword and run me through, so that these uncircumcised dogs may not come and taunt me and make sport of me." But the armor-bearer refused to strike Yahweh's anointed, and Saul staggered upright in the raging sun and fell on his own sword. The Bible says, "When the armor-bearer saw that Saul was dead, he, too, fell on his sword and died with him. Thus they all died together on that day, Saul, his three sons, and his armor-bearer, as well as his men."

The next day, the Philistines found Saul and cut off his head. The Bible says, "They deposited his armor in the temple of Ashtoreth and nailed his body on the wall of Beth-Shan." The implacable prophecy of Samuel's ghost was fulfilled. But the people of Jabesh-Gilead had not forgotten the savior of their eyes. The Bible says, "When the inhabitants of Jabesh-Gilead heard what the Philistines had done to Saul, the bravest of them journeyed together all night long and recovered the bodies of Saul and his sons from the wall of Beth-Shan; they brought them back to Jabesh and anointed them there with spices. Then they took their bones and buried them under the tamarisk tree in Jabesh and fasted for seven days."

Saul and his brave sons have been dust now for almost three millennia, but desperate mortals still seek prophecy from the ghosts of the dead and hear doom pronounced on tomorrow. Our ghosts speak in the new vision of our history, and in recent years Americans have searched out a diabolical vision of our past that rises from the grave to damn the future. Two extremes have somehow come together in the same midnight to listen to the same prophecy.

On the one hand, the Reaganites tell us in effect that America has been historically great because it has been historically greedy; in the last months they have pronounced doom on the national aspirations we once had to clothe the naked, to feed the hungry, to bind up the wounds of the fallen, and to care for the widow and orphan among us. They have discovered that it is not American to care for such things.

But we also have those other folks preaching with bullhorns in Harvard Square on Saturday morning, who believe that our past has been nothing but two centuries of infamy. Now even liberals languish for lack of purpose because we all know that Abraham Lincoln was a racist, Franklin Roosevelt was a politician, and Woodrow Wilson was a Presbyterian. Not long ago a dear friend of mine told me that American attitudes toward the Jews were no better than the Germans' because, given the historical circumstances, we might have had a holocaust, too. The fact that we did not have a holocaust did not make any difference to her.

The obvious conclusion for both these views of the past is doom for the future of justice in this society. The Reaganites and the radicals alike hear the voices of the dead in the night and conclude that anything we do for the people as a whole will finally be judged as contemptuously as we now judge the past. So we may as well eat, drink, and be merry—or, in the present jargon, wrap narcissism around ourselves and call it fate. How strange to such people Saul must be, standing bravely in the blazing sun with his back against a mountain, fighting to the end against the overpowering Philistines and killing himself before he would let them dishonor him.

Only a fool would deny that this diabolical past pronouncing doom speaks the truth; but it is not the whole truth. Saul did die as Samuel's ghost promised, but Saul in his life preserved his people, and they endured beyond his death and endure yet— something that might not have happened without him.

We shall certainly die, and we may not win any memorable triumphs in the daunting human struggle to do unselfish good. Our labors for justice will always be corrupted by our nature—as Saul's temper corrupted him. Yet corruption is not depravity, and frail human beings may still honor the good by giving a life and perhaps a death for it. We do remember Saul after all these centuries, and David loved him though Saul had tried to kill him.

There is always a party of hope and a party of despair. Now the party of hope that has always represented the America of our best dreams staggers before the cynicism of the right and the left who have read their history at midnight and hear a murmur of doom for generous aspiration. We could use Saul's courage against our gentle hopes.

When Samuel's ghost uttered his prophecy, Saul might have fled and hidden himself in the pleasures of some remote, private life. Instead he went into battle for his people—and we remember him. We might also imitate him, for there is a softer voice to history than the harsh pronouncements of our hard prophets. It tells us that tomorrow's doom may be but a step along the journey and that hope knows something other than endless defeat.

King Saul and the Witch of En-dor

Now Samuel was dead, and all Israel had lamented him, and buried him in Ramah, even in his own city. And Saul had put away those that had familiar spirits, and the wizards out of the land.

And the Philistines gathered themselves together, and came and pitched in Shunem, and Saul gathered all Israel together, and they pitched in Gilboa.

And when Saul saw the host of the Philistines, he was afraid, and his heart greatly trembled.

Different message with same scriptural text as the previous sermon. No place or date identified.

And when Saul enquired of the Lord, the Lord answered him not, neither by dreams, nor by Urim, nor by prophets.

Then said Saul unto his servants, Seek me a woman that hath a familiar spirit, that I may go to her, and enquire of her. And his servants said to him, Behold there is a woman that hath a familiar spirit at En-dor.

And Saul disguised himself, and put on other raiment, and he went, and two men with him, and they came to the woman by night, and he said, I pray thee, divine unto me by the familiar spirit, and bring me him up whom I shall name unto thee.

And the woman said unto him, Behold, thou knowest what Saul hath done, how he hath cut off those that hath familiar spirits, and the wizards out of the land. Wherefore then layest thou a snare for my life, to cause me to die?

And Saul sware to her by the Lord, saying, As the Lord liveth, there shall be no punishment happen to thee for this thing.

Then said the woman, Whom shall I bring up unto thee? And he said, Bring me up Samuel.

And when the woman saw Samuel, she cried with a loud voice, and the woman spake to Saul saying, Why has thou deceived me? For thou art Saul.

And the king said unto her, Be not afraid: for what sawest thou? And the woman said unto Saul, I saw gods ascending out of the earth.

And he said unto her, What form is he of? And she said, An old man cometh up, and he is covered with a mantle. And Saul perceived that it was Samuel, and he stooped with his face to the ground, and bowed himself.

And Samuel said to Saul, Why hast thou disquieted me, to bring me up? And Saul answered, I am sore distressed, for the Philistines make war against me and God is departed from me and answereth me no more, neither by prophets, nor by dreams. Therefore I have called thee, that thou mayest make known to me what I shall do.

Then said Samuel, Wherefore then dost thou ask of me, seeing the Lord is departed from thee and is become thine enemy?

And the Lord hath done to him as he spake by me for the Lord hath rent the kingdom out of thine hand, and given it to thy neighbor, even to David.

Because thou obeyest not the voice of the Lord, nor executedst his fierce wrath upon Amalek, therefore hath the Lord done this thing unto thee this day.

Moreover the Lord will also deliver Israel with thee into the hand of the Philistines, and tomorrow shalt thou and thy sons be with me. The Lord also shall deliver the host of Israel into the hand of the Philistines.

Then Saul fell straightway all along on the earth and was sore afraid because of the words of Samuel, and there was no strength in him, for he had had no bread all the day nor all the night. (I Samuel 28:3–20)

When I was a child, I read the Bible, especially the Old Testament, with the thrill others took in reading tales of magic and adventure in exotic places. This is an authentic ghost story that lives for me even yet every time I read it. In all three of my novels and in the fourth that I am writing now, the witch of En-dor gets a mention.

Here is Saul, Israel's first king, facing Philistine armies gathered against him and feeling the profound and terrifying silence of God. All else having failed, he asks for a witch, although as a servant king to Yahweh, he has tried to extirpate witchcraft from Israel. But the demand for witchcraft remained obviously high enough to stimulate a black market in magic, and his servants tell him of the witch at En-dor. "En," or "Ain," is the Hebrew word for a spring of water gushing out of the ground. In the arid lands of the eastern Mediterranean, a stream of water was a natural place for spirits to gather, and the witch at En-dor had her spiritual sisters at the spring of Castalia at Dephi in Greece, where another oracle foretold the future to those who came seeking it and had the money to pay for her visions.

In my mother's family the witch of En-dor caused some argument. My mother believed in evil spirits. She was horrified once when I came home from a friend's house saying we had played with a Ouija board and that it had told me I would spend my life in Brazil. Mother called the mother of my friend and told her that Ouija board was demonic, and the friend's mother promptly destroyed it. But Mother was much opposed to the idea that a witch could have brought the ghost of Samuel back from the dead. In her theological mode Mother pointed out that the witch shrieked when she saw Samuel's ghost, proving that she did not expect it. God used the occasion, Mother said, to send Samuel back from the dead to give Saul a message of doom, and the witch was as surprised as anybody.

But my aunt Bess had another opinion. She thought demons had all sorts of powers and that they thronged the world. Over and over again all her long life she told with a shudder of awe how she had been sitting in our woods one summer afternoon after my grandmother had died. Aunt Bess was sunk in grief, and suddenly she heard a clear, bell-like voice speak to her from behind. "If you turn around," the voice said, "you will see your mother." Aunt Bess said she thrilled with joy and started to turn around to see her mother when she remembered the witch of En-dor. If she looked around, she would be in the hands of Satan, and she knew she would perish as Saul perished in battle the day after his consultation with the witch. So she cried out, "Get thee behind me, Satan," and when she turned around, a miracle had happened. Nothing was there. She sat alone amid the droning peace of the summer woods.

My mother remained a skeptic, both about the powers of witches and about her sister Bess. But for years I thought that our woods was a magic and dangerous place where a voice might speak to me from an invisible source. I did not even consider for a long time a certain illogic that you have surely noticed in Aunt Bess's story. She said, "Get thee behind me, Satan," when Satan was already behind her. But she was only repeating the formula that Jesus had used when he was tempted of the devil in the wilderness. "Get thee behind me, Satan," was the conventional greeting for the occasional demon, whether it stood in front of you or behind you when you met.

Anyway, the story tells us that Saul was awash in the silence of God on the eve of battle with the Philistines, the deadliest enemies of Israel. Yahweh, the god of Israel, had cast him off. Why? The answer is troubling. Saul had been guilty of a deed of mercy. Not only that, he lied about what he had done to Samuel, the designated chief prophet of God in Israel. Samuel and Saul did not get along.

I suspect a major reason was jealousy. Samuel had been head prophet and judge in Israel since his youth. God had private conversations with him, and he told the Israelites what God had said. But then he got old. He tried to pass on his sacred position to his two sons. Unfortunately they were corrupt and incompetent. Besides that, Israel was surrounded by enemies with a thirst for blood. Samuel had some success in fighting them off with incantations and sacrifices, but the peril remained. The Israelites demanded a king who could lead soldiers into battle and win. Since Samuel was Yahweh's chief agent, the Israelites demanded that he find them a king.

Samuel and God were both annoyed by this demand. God instructed Samuel to give the people a lecture on the dangers of big government, and he did. A king would draft sons into the army, tax their land, corrupt wives, and enslave the masses. The stubborn people persisted in their clamor for a king. God and Samuel reluctantly gave them Saul.

Saul was the son of a wealthy farmer in the tribe of Benjamin down in the South. He was a big guy. The Bible tells us a couple of times that he was the tallest man in Israel, standing a head above anybody else in the country. Three asses strayed from his father's place. He and a friend went off to find them. After three days of fruitless search they decided to consult Samuel, who had a reputation as a seer. Seers were good at finding lost things. They were not disappointed. On his side Samuel took one look at Saul, and he and Yahweh jointly decided that this was the king the people needed.

Saul did not want to be king. He went into some sort of babbling trance after Samuel poured oil on his head to certify his divine election. He refused to tell his family what had happened. When Samuel summoned Israel together to introduce them to their king, Saul ran off and hid among the baggage people had brought to the assembly. Somebody led him out, and the people acclaimed him. But many Israelites doubted. What could anybody expect of a man who didn't want the job? But like many politicians, Saul discovered that power suited him. He began slaughtering Israel's enemies, and he had such success that his approval rating rose dramatically in the polls. His sons were great fighters, too, and very soon even the mighty Philistines were on the run. Moreover, Saul was a devout worshiper of Yahweh, raised up altars to him, and made life hot for idolaters. His motto might have been "All the way with Yahweh," and Samuel should have been pleased.

But Samuel was not pleased. He clashed repeatedly with Saul and his sons. It looks very much to me as if the fading older man was jealous of the younger man's startling success and popularity. The final straw was Saul's treatment of the Amalekites, who were living peacefully as Israel's neighbors. Samuel recalled that, during the Exodus a couple of centuries before, the ancestors of these Amalekites had harassed the Israelites on their way from Egypt to Palestine, the promised land. Samuel ordered Saul to go fight them. "Go now and fall upon the Amalekites and destroy them, and put their property under ban. Spare no one; put them all to death, men and women, children and babes in arms, herds and flocks, camels and asses."

Here is the prophet of a tribal god urging destruction down to the last baby in arms. It was a repetition of the commands Yahweh had given Joshua when Israel crossed the Jordan. I should say that my mother was a kind and gentle person, endowed with a fine sense of humor, but she had no difficulty with Samuel's earlier command that Saul destroy every man, woman, and child among the Amalekites. In all fairness we should probably say that none of the gods in the region was inferior to Yahweh in viciousness towards enemies in war. The petty kings of Palestine and Syria have left their proud boasts of cruelty in the names of their gods carved on many a stone that survives from those misty regions of time.

Anyway, Saul dutifully went out and slaughtered Amalekites. Both they and their property were supposed to be devoted to God—that is, they were to be exterminated. But for some reason he kept Agag, king of the Amalekites, alive, and he did not destroy the best of the livestock. The Bible does not tell us why he spared Agag. Maybe it was professional courtesy. Saul parceled the captured livestock out among his soldiers as a reward for valor. Any of us would have done the same. Why burn a good fat cow to cinders when you can make her the centerpiece of an outdoor barbecue?

Naturally God knew about this disobedience right away and sent Samuel hustling to Gilgal, where Saul was camped. Samuel was furious. Prophets in all the ages are furious, but Samuel was enraged. Saul made excuses. He said he planned to sacrifice *some* of the animals to Yahweh. But Samuel pointed out that he was supposed to sacrifice them all. Samuel thundered back one of the great sentences of the Bible, often quoted by preachers in my boyhood:

> Obedience is better than sacrifice, and to listen to him [that is, God] than the fat of rams.
> Defiance of him is sinful as witchcraft, yielding to men as evil as idolatry.

King Saul and the Witch of En-dor

Because you have rejected the word of the Lord, the Lord has rejected you as king.

Saul was crushed. He tried to make up with Samuel. Samuel turned away. Saul in despair grabbed Samuel's cloak so that it tore, and Samuel said, "The Lord has torn the kingdom of Israel from your hand today and will give it to another, a better man than you." Then Samuel commanded that Agag be brought out, and the prophet of God cut the Amalekite king in pieces before God. The wording of the biblical text makes it seem as if Samuel made a human sacrifice of Agag to Yahweh, and that, after all, is what it meant to put people under the divine ban.

So young David became the next in line to the throne. Saul became the first historical figure we know to have endured bouts of clinical depression. And so it was that, on the eve of a great battle for his life and Israel's, he was forsaken by God. That is why he found himself in the house of a witch in the dead of night, seeking Samuel's ghost to tell him what to do. Samuel's ghost duly appeared, irascible as ever, and repeated his prophecy of doom on Saul and all his house: "Tomorrow, thou and thy sons shall be with me." That is, they would be dead. And so it was.

Now what are we to make of all this? We might be free to make nothing of it at all except that our democracy nowadays is threatened by religious fundamentalists who make a great deal of stories like this. They want us to accept the Bible as our basic standard of science, morals, and family values. School boards in Texas and other bizarre places proclaim that something called "creationism" taken out of the Bible has the same validity as evolutionary biology taken out of laboratories and scientific observation and measurement. Textbook companies are forced to pander to such beliefs if they are to get their books adopted by many southern states. The Southern Baptists recently decreed that women should be submissive to their husbands because the Bible teaches that men are to rule the family. Southern Baptists have thus far not come out in favor of polygamy, although polygamy was the rule of the Hebrew Bible, and it is nowhere forbidden in the New Testament.

So why not believe in literal witches? What do we do with the witch of En-dor? Biblical literalists such as Pat Robertson unabashedly hold that this text proves that witches do exist with occult powers and that they are dangerous to life and faith. I am sure they believe also that many of these witches are Unitarians. How could it be otherwise if the Bible is their rule? Martin Luther believed in witchcraft all his life, preached against witches, and sometimes pointed out this or that witch in his congregation. He thought witches should be put to death. In 1540 three witches were burned at the stake in Wittenberg, a woman fifty years old and two young men, one her son. We don't know Luther's role in their deaths, but nothing we know that he said or wrote allows us to think he would have objected to their death by fire.

Something essential is at stake here. John Wesley made an astute point against the Age of Reason of the eighteenth century when he lived. He said this: "The giving up of witchcraft is, in effect, the giving up of the Bible." If only one account of what he called "the intercourse of men with . . . spirits be admitted," he said, Deism, Atheism, and Materialism all fall to the ground. He had a point. If we take the Bible literally, witches may be all around us, and the "modern" world we think we know may be an illusion.

Springs of water along the Mediterranean shore have astonishing longevity. On hot days I have drunk from the cold water of Castalia on the side of Mt. Parnassus at Delphi and hope to again. Perhaps under a different name the spring of En-dor still rushes out of the depths of the earth, and the spirits that inhabit it may today live in some Arab woman who can summon up the dead to tell us the future if we only go to her by night.

But none of us here believes such a thing, and put to the test even the Ralph Reeds, the Pat Robertsons, the Jerry Falwells, and the Trent Lotts of earth are much more likely to consult their stockbrokers to see the future than they are to seek out a witch by night. The story of the witch of En-dor is obviously a legend born of folk tales intended to explain a calamity—the death of Saul at the hands of the Philistines. Someone wrote it down, and the sage scholars who put the Hebrew Bible together many centuries after Saul had perished wove it into their narrative to show that when Israel obeyed Yahweh, the people were preserved from conquest, but when Israel disobeyed, the people fell into servitude to foreigners.

The story proved to be too good to clean up entirely. The witch of En-dor turns out to be a nice person. When Samuel has delivered his dreadful message and Saul has fainted, she and Saul's aides lift him up, give him food and drink, and make him rest. She demonstrates decency and compassion. So we have a wonderful tale, more vivid in its way than the tales of Homer in *The Iliad* and *The Odyssey,* for Saul stands forth as a human personality much more vividly than does Achilles or Hector or Odysseus. When we look at the books of Joshua, Judges, Ruth, Samuel, and Kings, all done by the same writer or school of writers, we are looking at the Shakespeare of the ancient world.

But we do not have people among us telling us that we should direct our foreign and domestic policy by texts from Shakespeare. The Bible is a different order of literature, and we Unitarians do not pay enough attention to it. We take it for granted that liberal people like ourselves do not need to bother with such stuff. This attitude seems to be as smug and narrow-minded as the notion that we don't have to think much about the school system in Boston because we live in Belmont or that those of us who are not gay do not have to worry about the AIDS virus.

The Bible is a repository of the human experience of searching for God over centuries of time. It has lessons for us. One of the most important is that religion is glorious when it seeks and horrible when it finds. The God of the text that I have read to you this morning has a magnetic appeal to people as diverse as Pat Robertson and the fanatical Israeli settlers on the West Bank who believe that this God has promised them and their children all of Palestine regardless of what claims centuries of habitation may have given to the Arabs who live there. We are the Amalekites to Pat Robertson; the Arabs are the Amalekites to those Israeli settlers in Hebron and other places who now block peace in the Middle East. The God of my text today is convenient because He sanctifies the most evil impulses of the human heart.

But there is another God in the Bible—the God of second Isaiah, Amos, and Joel, the God who is more distant, more mysterious, more unapproachable, and yet more benign. That God is the God of all the earth who plants within us an impulse to do good to one another and to seek peace rather than war in the search for a vision that is always deferred. That God makes us aspire to the ever-receding hope of the day when, as Joel said, "Every man shall sit under his own vine and fig tree, and none shall make them afraid."

That God is always to be sought and neither in the dead of night in voices from the grave summoned by witchcraft nor in the certitudes of television preachers and politicians who come to us in bright lights and cosmetics and hair spray and genial voices conveying the religious craziness of the moment. We are reluctant as Unitarians to criticize other faiths. But in this day I do not think we owe courtesy to the maligned ghost of Samuel the prophet wherever he speaks his barbarous message. Like Saul, most of us live in the silence of God. The difficulty of our task is to accept that silence as a voice and to fill it with the voices of a world of demand, duty, and opportunity that still speaks though God is quiet.

[The Marriage at Cana]

And on the third day there was a marriage in Cana of Galilee; and the mother of Jesus was there:

And both Jesus was called, and his disciples, to the marriage.

And when they wanted wine, the mother of Jesus saith unto him, They have no wine.

Jesus saith unto her, Woman, what have I to do with thee? mine hour is not yet come.

His mother saith unto the servants, Whatsoever he saith unto you, do it.

Delivered at Morning Prayers, Appleton Chapel, Memorial Church, Harvard University, Spring 1989.

And there were set there six waterpots of stone, after the manner of the
purifying of the Jews, containing two
or three firkins apiece.

Jesus saith unto them, Fill the
waterpots with water. And they filled
them up to the brim.

And he saith unto them, Draw out
now, and bear unto the governor of the
feast. And they bare it.

When the ruler of the feast had
tasted the water that was made wine,
and knew not whence it was: (but the
servants which drew the water knew;)
the governor of the feast called the
bridegroom.

And saith unto him, Every man
at the beginning doth set forth good
wine; and when men have well drunk,
then that which is worse: but thou
hast kept the good wine until now.

This beginning of miracles
did Jesus in Cana of Galilee, and manifested forth his glory, and his disciples believed on him. (John 2:1–11)

The Fourth Gospel is my favorite of the accounts we have of the
life of Jesus. Tradition ascribes it to John the apostle, but the tradition is very late and apparently the gospel is late, too—some sev-
enty years after the first Easter. We don't know who wrote it.

We can know some things about the writer. He knew the religion of the Jews, and he also knew the common Greek culture that
embraced the eastern Mediterranean under the imperial control
of the Pax Romana. He calls Christ the logos—showing that he
understood something of Greek philosophy that made the logos
the principle of rationality in the universe, the quality that makes
it orderly and knowable.

But he also knew Greek mythology. Here in this wonderful tale
of the changing of the water into wine at the wedding of Cana in

Galilee, we pick up an echo of the cult of Dionysus. He was the god of wine, and one of his powers was to change water into wine. He came to be the god of fertility, causing seeds to germinate and animals to bear young. He was also the god of the arts, what we might call the god of the creative imagination. His wine was the symbol of those spontaneous human qualities that lie beyond the power of reason to comprehend or manipulate, those qualities that are a gift.

Sometimes Dionysus was worshiped with great solemnity, but we are more familiar with the orgiastic rites where his worshipers abandoned themselves to sexual license.

In this story, Christ shows all the good qualities of Dionysus but within the decorous circumstances of a wedding. He thus sanctifies marriage and sex without blessing orgies or drunkenness. When this gospel was written, many fanatics in the Greek world had pushed the opposition of soul and body to the point that sex was thought to be wicked, the act that imprisoned more souls in more bodies. The Christ at the wedding in Cana and throughout the Gospel of John tells us that the natural state of humankind is in a body and that bodies are just fine because God created them. "Without him was not anything made that was made."

My aunt Bess and my aunt Bert and my aunt Nelle worked hard to explain this story away. They couldn't imagine Jesus made wine; they said he made grape juice. The reason the master of the feast liked Jesus' wine so much, they said, was that it was alcohol free. I recall one summer as a young teenager riding home to Tennessee with Aunt Bert and Aunt Bess after spending a few weeks with them in Philadelphia, where they lived. It was the epoch of the two-lane highway and the nondescript roadside shack that sold greasy food. Aunt Bert loved to stride into such places and demand, "Do you serve beer?" More often than not the owner would say, "Sure, lady. What kind do you want?" That gave Aunt Bert a theatrical opportunity to declare, "Well, *we* don't eat in places that serve beer!" Thereupon, she would turn on her heel and walk out, expecting—I think—the agonized owner to come rushing after her, pleading, "Lady, if you will only eat my bacon and eggs, I'll never serve beer again in my life." It never happened.

We went all day without food, and by the time we arrived that night at my cousin Beryl's farm in upper East Tennessee, I was ready to gnaw the tops off my shoes.

My mother never fell into such foolishness. She had, after all, married a Greek, and my father had a vineyard and made wine, allowing Aunt Bert, Aunt Bess, and Aunt Nelle much opportunity for quiet self-righteousness. My father's family in Greece interpreted this text differently. I recall summer nights decades ago sitting with my uncle John on the terrace of the family home in Piraeus, looking out over the dark of the Bay of Faliron to Athens where the Acropolis gleamed under the moon. When my aunt Polyxene would yell at him, "You're drinking too much," Uncle John would lift his glass in the dimness and say in drunken reverence, "Christ made it; we should drink it." I think Uncle John imagined Christ wearing the garlands of ivy that Dionysus wore about his head.

Uncle John drank too much, but I think he had the right idea. Here in this story is Christ at a wedding, obviously enjoying himself, a little annoyed with his mother for pushing him into doing miracles before he was ready, but finally succumbing to her desire to please people she cared for.

This is a good time of year. Exams are just about over, and graduation is near, and we can feel all around us in the Yard the anticipations of endings and new beginnings. Our beloved Peter Gomes will, of course, preach another of his witty and profound baccalaureate sermons, and most of us will feel the religious solemnity of this moment of sublime transformation, a time for reflection.

But it is also a time for high-spirited celebration. Perhaps the greatest message of this story is that God's benediction lies also in our less restrained moments, in the worldly joy, the victorious release that comes from finishing hard work, from pausing at the entryway to another room in life. In the world of Dionysus and Christ, wine was the symbol of that part of life that is uncontrolled, the gift of creation, of being. We are alive, bountifully alive, sharing life with one another, this time, this gift, this grace. We can rejoice together in that wine that the Psalmist tells us "maketh glad the heart of man"—and woman, too.

[Beauty]

O sing unto the Lord a new song:
sing unto the Lord, all the earth.

Sing unto the Lord, bless his
name; shew forth his salvation from
day to day,

Declare his glory among the heathen, his wonder among all people.

For the Lord is great, and greatly
to be praised: he is to be feared above
all gods.

For all the gods of the nations are
idols: but the Lord made the heavens.

Honour and majesty are before
him: strength and beauty are in his
sanctuary.

Delivered at Harvard Divinity School, 8 November 1989, and at Morning Prayers, Appleton Chapel, Memorial Church, Harvard University, date unknown.

Give unto the Lord, o ye kindreds
of the people, give unto the Lord glory
and strength.
Give unto the Lord the glory due
unto his name: bring an offering, and
come into his courts.
O worship the Lord in the beauty
of holiness: fear before him, all the
earth.
Say among the heathen that the
Lord reigneth: the world also shall be
established that it shall not be moved:
he shall judge the people righteously.
Let the heavens rejoice, and let
the earth be glad; let the sea roar, and
the fulness thereof.
Let the field be joyful, and all that
is therein: then shall all the trees of
the wood rejoice
Before the Lord: for he cometh,
for he cometh to judge the earth: he
shall judge the world with righteousness, and the people with his truth.
(Psalm 96)

I am struck by how frequently beauty is mentioned in the Old
Testament and how rare even the concept is in the New. Our
morning Psalm shines with love of the beauty of the creation and
with the splendor of God Himself. The word "beauty" is scattered
throughout both historical and poetic books of the Hebrew canon.

Christians have adopted these books and these sentiments,
and it is a good thing, for in the New Testament the word "beauty"
does not appear at all. The word "beautiful" appears twice as the
name of a gate in Jerusalem, once as an allegory for hypocrisy,
and once in the metaphorical utterance of Paul in Romans 10:15:
"How beautiful are the feet of them that preach the gospel of
peace, and bring glad tidings of good things." Nowhere in the
New Testament do I find any sense that the earth itself is beautiful and that we should rejoice in it. Only the Book of Revelation

captures something of the majesty of God's creation, but that majesty is in the vision of what is yet to be, the new heavens and the new earth, the New Jerusalem. The rest of the New Testament seems bent on preparing people to reject the earth because it is bound by time and passing away. "Here," the author of Hebrews said, "we have no continuing city, but we seek one to come."

Christians have always had trouble with the temporary beauties of creation. The acceptance of a creator God requires us to pledge formal assent to the goodness of creation, but we have never been easy about it. This summer my wife Lanier and I bicycled from Bordeaux to Carcassonne, pedaling through the heart of the French Cathar country of the Middle Ages.

The Cathars represented the greatest medieval dissent from the Catholic Church and the doctrine of creation that has always caused Christians so much trouble. They believed in two gods, one the bad, dark god who had made the world of matter—the world we inhabit—and the other the bright, good god who created the world of immaterial light. In the twelfth century they numbered tens of thousands of followers in the South of France. Unable to subdue them by the preaching of the Dominicans, the Church launched a merciless crusade against them, and in 1243 a remnant of Cathars made a futile last stand in a castle atop Montsegur. The Catholic army battered down the walls with catapults and led 207 survivors down from the mountain to be burned alive on a huge bonfire.

Montsegur stands there yet, a conical peak in the Pyrenees looming above the lush green valley of the River Aude. The last approach was too steep for middle-aged people like ourselves to pull, and so we pushed the bikes four miles on a serpentine road, climbing through upland meadows under a soft blue sky, hearing the irregular clangor of cowbells. Leaving our wheels at a parking area, we ascended the rest of the way on a rocky path to the ruins of a later chateau that replaced the broken Cathar fortress. Despite the warning of the Michelin guide that those subject to vertigo should stay off the walls, I crept up a rickety steel ladder and stood uncertainly in the wind looking out on the greater peaks above and the valley that plunged away beneath my feet to the giddy distance. I sympathized with the Cathars, but as I drank in their last view of earth, I thought, "How could they have said that this was not beautiful?"

Many scholars have pointed out that the Cathars only took to an extreme the general distaste for the created world normal for most Christian theologians. Christianity seems so purposeful, so intent on getting from here to there, that it has had little patience for those who want to sanctify the moment as a thing unto itself. Like the Catholics who killed them, the Cathars were quite willing to kill in the name of the world that lay beyond this world, the immaterial city not made with hands. Can we be Christians and not be on pilgrimage? Must we always be pressing on?

Wallace Stevens in his poem "Sunday Morning" sets the Christian opposition between this world and the next:

> Is there no change of death in paradise?
> Does ripe fruit never fall? Or do the boughs
> Hang always heavy in that perfect sky,
> Unchanging, yet so like our perishing earth,
> With rivers like our own that seek for seas
> They never find, the same receding shores
> That never touch with inarticulate pang?
> . . .
> Death is the mother of beauty, mystical,
> Within whose burning bosom we devise
> Our earthly mothers waiting, sleeplessly.

Stevens feels nostalgia and longing for the timeless heaven that has become a myth to the woman who takes her coffee late on a Sunday morning with only the hint of an old religious consciousness at the border of her mind. Twice in the poem he repeats the line, "Death is the mother of beauty," to say to us (I think) that we could have no sense of earthly beauty unless we knew that time was taking it away. Time washes through a sensual world where we enjoy the sight, the feel, the taste, the smell, the sound of life in motion—all dear to us just because we know we cannot hold it or stop it. For the Greeks the word *oraios* meaning "beauty" is a cognate of the word *ora* meaning a limited time, the word from which we take our word "hour." Could there be beauty if all were frozen in a changeless paradise, or would paradise be a bore? The question represents a contradiction within our faith that goes back to its founding.

I believe that scripture and tradition are alike texts for our theology. Our tradition instructs us that a preoccupation with life as pilgrimage, relentlessly moving to something else, time seeking eternity at every moment, searching for paradise after death, or even seeking endlessly for some timeless goal at the end of progress in this world, finally devastates the very faith it seeks to express. We affirm that God created the earth we have and the heaven we do not. And yet we often reject the physical now, the mysterious and outflowing present we have but like flowing water cannot clutch in our hands, for some immaterial part of creation yet to come.

We live in a world called Harvard that always hurries us on to an ever-receding beyond, that tells us to spend time and not to waste it, to get our next degree or write our next book. Harvard is an eschatological experience, always looking to the end of time rather than to the joys of time itself.

Let us see time not as a coin to be spent for something else but each moment as treasure in itself to contemplate and love. God has created the future, and we are bound to look to it. But He has created the present, too, and we are lost if we do not live in it. Said the Psalmist, "This is the day which the Lord hath made: we will rejoice and be glad in it."

Remarks on Rosh Hashanah

O sing unto the Lord a new song;
for he hath done marvelous things; his
right hand, and his holy arm, hath gotten him the victory.

The Lord hath made known his salvation; his righteousness hath he openly
shewed in the sight of the heathen.

He hath remembered his mercy
and his truth toward the house of
Israel: all the ends of the earth have
seen the salvation of our God. (Psalms
98:1–3)

Delivered at Morning Prayers, Appleton Chapel, Memorial Church, Harvard
University, date unknown. Published in *Best Sermons 5*. Ed. James W. Cox
(San Francisco: Harper, 1992), 67–69.

This is Rosh Hashanah, the Jewish new year. Christians finally adopted the Roman custom of beginning the new year in January. I think we missed a great opportunity by not taking up the Jewish custom of beginning it now. I for one can tell little difference between December and January, at least here in Massachusetts. They are both cold and miserable, and although January is named for Janus, the Roman god of beginnings, it is a month when much of life seems almost to cease or to slow to a dead crawl.

But in September or early October when Rosh Hashanah comes, there seems to be a quickening in the earth. Here in our university the mood of renewal is strong. I never get over my simple joy at seeing the Yard fill up with students after its August emptiness and at greeting my colleagues back from their summer dispersions, ready to take up again our rituals and routines of teaching and learning and simply being together in this community. There always comes a morning—it has come early this year—when I push my bicycle out into the street and realize that the maple tree in front of my house is already turning red, that there is a sharpness in the air portending autumn, and that I have to go back into the house and put on a windbreaker before I pedal to my office. On that morning I am ready to begin a new year.

Our faith, in both its Jewish and Christian manifestations, takes pleasure in new beginnings. They are taken to be a sign that God is still with his people. The rejoicing at a new start is all the greater because of an earlier fear that perhaps we are alone and that God had forsaken us. So it is with the familiar Psalm that I have read to you this morning: "O sing unto the Lord a new song; for he hath done marvelous things: his right hand, and his holy arm, hath gotten him the victory."

Why sing a new song? Because God has led his people back to Jerusalem after captivity and exile in Babylon. The old songs were of distance, of unsatisfied yearning: "O Lord: keep not silence: O Lord, be not far from me." The new song is of victory, return, a new beginning in the land of promise, and in the new beginning is the hand of God.

The Bible abounds with such new beginnings. Abraham goes out from Ur to a new covenant in a new land; the oppressed Israelites make their exodus from Egypt, the land of bondage, and make a new start in the land of promise. And the New Testament is yet another new beginning. "Therefore if any man be in Christ," Paul wrote to the Corinthians, "he is a new creature: old things are passed away; behold, all things are become new."

And yet for both Christians and Jews, there is a paradox here. The new in the Bible is always seen not as something *utterly* new but as a step on the way back to the pristine and original state of the old. The covenant with Abraham and the testament of Christ both look back to Eden and the conviction of Jews and Christians alike that God created this world neither by accident nor aberration but for some good purpose. The new song that our psalmist sings in the text of the morning is of return to the old holy city of David, Jerusalem the golden—a new start in an old place sanctified by an ancient promise. God is in the new start because he was also in the older beginning that provided the materials from which the new start might be made and shaped. He is in the new year because he was also in the old.

Every new academic year represents a new start. Here a new class comes gingerly into Harvard Yard, many of its members sure that they got here by accident, because some fool on the admissions committee nodded. But, in fact, they are here for this new beginning because of a past life that has added up to something. Their faculty members will teach them traditions from the past seen in the light of new books, new theories, new discoveries. A university exists, it seems to me, to preserve, to revere, and to pass on the old through the continual transformations of new beginnings. Education is a living process of eternal return.

Yes, there *is* something perverse in human nature or perhaps in the nature of things that makes our products fall short of our plans and at times fatigues us so that like the world-weary writer of the Book of Ecclesiastes we may lament: "The thing that hath been, it is that which shall be; and that which is done is that which shall be done; and there is no new thing under the sun."

Yet our faith that creation is fundamentally good means that we can labor within it in the trust that something good from our work will endure to provide the material for a new start someday. Our hope at new beginnings is a reaffirmation of the faith that we have inherited something worth transforming. And so I wish for you all a happy new year and new songs to sing in its new days.

[Faith and Doubt]

> My God, my God, why hast thou
> forsaken me? Why art thou so far from
> helping me, and from the words of my
> roaring?
> O my god, I cry in the daytime,
> but thou hearest not; and in the night
> season, and am not silent.
> But thou art holy, O thou that
> inhabitest the praises of Israel. (Psalm
> 22:1–3)

This has been a week for reflection on the difficult proposition that our lives mean something. April 19 was the fiftieth anniversary of the uprising in the Warsaw Ghetto where the Jews fought back against the German campaign to exterminate them. Yesterday the Holocaust Museum opened in Washington to preserve the

Delivered at Morning Prayers, Appleton Chapel, Memorial Church, Harvard University, 23 April 1993.

vivid memory of those who died in violent dignity rather than submit to the methodical Nazi final solution.

On the same day that we remembered the Warsaw Uprising, David Koresh and his band of religious fanatics in Waco, Texas, committed mass suicide by fire.

Confronted by the Holocaust, many Jews lost their faith. The very banality of evil that Hannah Arendt identified in the mindless functionaries who set the railroad schedules for trainloads of Jews going to the death camps is enough to shake to the foundations all easy expressions of religious belief by anyone who accepts faith in a personal god.

David Koresh's cult seems on the surface to have been the opposite of doubt. He claimed to be God himself or at least the Messiah, and his doomed followers professed faith to the death in him. They acted on their faith. Contrary to the expectations of the FBI, David Koresh and his disciples did not surrender when tear gas was pumped in. They burned themselves alive.

I find in these two radically different events a connection that I want to ponder for a moment.

The Holocaust is a horror that calls into question any belief in God whose eye is on the sparrow. And yet as events in this terrible century call faith into question, fundamentalist sects arise to shout at us that there is no doubt at all.

I grew up in a fundamentalist religion not as fanatical as that of David Koresh and his band. But it was equally hostile to any questioning of belief.

When I was a child, my mother took her children to the Methodist church in a rural community called Martel near our farm. I loved the Martel church because we shared a minister with another church, and that meant we had preaching only twice a month.

But one Sunday at dinner over the obligatory fried chicken, a brash young minister named James Shugart from Emory University got into a vehement theological argument with my mother. Mother knew the Bible by heart, and she overwhelmed him with a barrage of scriptural quotations. Finally, in defeat and exasperation, Mr. Shugart blurted out, "Well, Mrs. Marius, Jesus made SOME mistakes."

Mother never went to the Methodist church again.

We started walking up the hill to the Midway Baptist Church, whose graveyard adjoined one of our pastures. In the Midway Baptist Church, Jesus made no mistakes.

My mother's life was given over to protecting her children and, I believe, herself from losing faith in God. I came to realize that my mother, her sisters, and other fundamentalists were consumed with doubt, that their faith was so fragile that it had to be protected like some artificial color from the brilliant sun.

I suspect that David Koresh's band was made up of people in desperate flight from the horrors of their own doubt within. And I suspect that the bitter hatred that Christians have directed against the Jews for nearly two thousand years is in truth a hatred of the doubts that Christians feel about their own faith. To persecute Jews allows Christians to think, "Yes, we do believe, after all. We have proved our faith by destroying those who do not share it." Few Christian Poles gave any help or sympathy to the Jews of the Ghetto. Indeed, many members of the Christian population rushed to the walls of the Ghetto to see the Jews destroyed by the Wehrmacht.

David Koresh's people "proved" their faith by dying in a fanatical funeral pyre. Better die than admit doubt.

But to profess faith—faith in God, faith in the notion that our lives mean something before the infinity or space and time, faith that benevolence is better than greed, that joy is possible in the soul—is always to admit that doubt lies in the shadows near at hand. We cannot say "I believe" without acknowledging that unbelief is possible.

It is a comfort to those of us who are religiously inclined to see unbelief sanctioned in the Psalms. "My God, my God why hast thou forsaken me?" cries our Psalmist of the morning. The Christians among us recognize that shout into the dark as the last words of Christ on the cross.

If the humanity of Christ means anything, it is that he felt himself utterly forsaken when he died the horrible death of a rebel under Roman law. I have often thought that if there was such a miracle as the resurrection, the most startled and astonished character in the drama must have been Christ himself, for if the incarnation means anything, the suffering and despair of the cross must have been real and final to the young man who hung there and died.

It is a difficult matter—to affirm meaning, to affirm faith in life and in its mysterious and hidden purposes and at the same time to acknowledge that, yes, there is doubt behind all our professions of faith. We are not this morning a community of certainty but a community of hope. That is what we should be. Our doubts define our faith; our faith and our doubts live together in a blessed union that we cannot break without becoming inhuman. At times we feel forsaken; but at other times we live in hope. That cycle is existence. We should greet it with joy.

[Lazarus]

> Then when Mary was come where
> Jesus was and saw him, she fell down
> at his feet, saying unto him, Lord, if
> thou hadst been here, my brother had
> not died.
> When Jesus therefore saw her
> weeping, and the Jews also weeping
> which came with her, he groaned in
> the spirit, and was troubled.
> And said, Where have
> ye laid him? They said unto him,
> Lord, come and see.
> Jesus wept. (John 11:32–35)

You recognize this story as the prologue to the resurrection of Lazarus at a place called Bethany. It is the greatest miracle recorded in the Fourth Gospel apart from the resurrection of Jesus

Delivered at Morning Prayers, Appleton Chapel, Memorial Church, Harvard University, 3 March 1994.

himself. The gospel we call John does not have many miracles, but the author makes them count and builds a crescendo from the turning of water into wine at the wedding at Cana in Galilee to the great Easter triumph. In the Greek text they are called signs.

Signs of what?

As it turns out, they are mostly signs that affirm the goodness of the physical life—not only changing that water to wine at a wedding where reproduction was to be expected but also healing the lame man at the pool of Bethesda, multiplying five loaves and two fishes to feed a multitude of five thousand, giving sight to a man blind from birth, and now this, raising the dead. The Fourth Gospel spoke to a world of Greek philosophy that tried to set body and soul in opposition to each other, and it said, in effect, "Just a minute. You can't separate the two. We don't *have* a body and soul; we *are* body and soul in one being."

This is the season of Lent when many devout Christians deny themselves some physical pleasure so they may think more profoundly on the death and resurrection of Christ. I don't think there's any harm to Lenten self-denial. But I have the feeling that the writer of the Fourth Gospel, resurrected in our day, might listen in good-natured perplexity to our explanations for Lent and shrug and lift his glass and say, "Well, I'll drink to that."

At any rate, here is Jesus confronted by the death of a good friend, and he doesn't act a bit like Socrates. He is not calm and self-possessed, and he does not say as people inevitably say at funerals in rural Tennessee, where I grew up, "He's not really dead; he's in heaven, and doesn't he look natural!" Led to the grave of Lazarus, Jesus wept.

It is a remarkable detail. Why did Jesus weep? Why did the writer of the Fourth Gospel remember or add that detail? Well, he's obviously hinting at the Greek philosophical notion that God is eternally still. The God of Greek philosophy is like a modern Republican looking at health care in America: he doesn't suffer a bit; he doesn't have any emotions at all. And Jesus wept.

Why? Didn't he know he was going to raise Lazarus from the dead? I have a videotape of a football game played a couple of years ago when Tennessee trailed Notre Dame thirty-one to seven and came back and won thirty-five to thirty-four. The tape is appropriately titled "Miracle in South Bend." I've watched it sometimes late at night. I drink a beer or two, and at the moment when the game seems hopeless, I don't weep. I chortle because I know victory is inevitable. No matter how many times I play that tape, I know the Volunteers are going to win.

Now didn't Jesus know that he was going to raise Lazarus? Talk about a come-from-behind victory! There it was, as inevitable as my videotape. A triumph over sin, death, and the devil should be at least marginally more satisfying than even beating Notre Dame coach Lou Holtz. But Jesus wept.

The church fathers were puzzled by this text. I don't know any of them who said Jesus wept because his friend Lazarus was dead. Some said Jesus wept for the unbelief he saw all around him in the people who loved him and whom he loved. The late-medieval commentator Denis the Carthusian summed up the patristic tradition: *Flevit Jesus Lazarum, non quia mortuus fuit . . .* (Jesus wept for Lazarus not because he was dead but because he was to be recalled to the pains of this life).

I dissent. It looks to me as if Jesus wept because Lazarus was dead. Confronted by death, even Jesus wavered and felt overwhelmed with grief.

It is a beautiful image for the religious person. We are swept today by claims to unflinching religious certainty. Last week Bernard Goldstein machine-gunned forty worshiping Arabs in a mosque in Palestine. A fundamentalist Christian is on trial at this moment in Florida for having gunned down an abortion doctor. Egypt is virtually closed to foreigners because fundamentalist Moslems kill tourists who violate the laws of the Koran. And the violence between Catholics and Protestants goes on.

Faith is a fragile and intangible business. In the New Testament at least it is very hard to tell the difference between faith and hope. Wherever anyone in the New Testament says, "I believe," a silent assumption stands behind the confession: Unbelief is possible. Belief and unbelief coexist in us all.

The Jesus in this story from the Fourth Gospel stands by the grave of a friend and weeps. It is a detail so striking that it remains in a tradition that, at the end of his little book, the writer of the gospel admits is heavily edited.

I like to think that Jesus himself provides the example for the way that faith and doubt are mixed up in any religious awareness that is honest and true. Our strongest faith is always dark with doubt. We do not prove our faith to others or to ourselves by hating them. Before death Jesus did not kill; Jesus wept.

[Jesus and Paul]

Several of my friends were sitting around with me the other night, talking about Jesus. We were not Jesus freaks or born again. On the contrary, one of us expressed her puzzlement at the place of Jesus in the Western tradition. Why does every age find in him the ideal of human perfection? The image of Jesus changes with the changes in what we consider valuable. Fritz Peterson, a former baseball player and present chaplain in the Major Leagues, was quoted the other day in the *New York Times* on the subject of Jesus: "I firmly believe that if Jesus Christ was sliding into second base, he would knock the second baseman into left field to break up the double play. Christ might not throw a spitball, but he would play hard within the rules." Mr. Peterson's view is a bit bizarre, but it is not out of keeping with what people have been doing to Jesus since classical times.

Delivered at Morning Prayers, Harvard University, date unknown.

I said that the reason we have always been able to make so much of Jesus is that we know so little about him. We don't know what he did for the first thirty years of his life. The three years of his ministry are clouded with mystery and legend. He appears as a miracle worker and as a prophet announcing the immediate advent of a kingdom of heaven that has not come in two thousand years. Unlike modern-day followers in the current president's administration, he had a lot to say about the virtues of the poor, and he said it was harder for a rich man to enter the kingdom than it was for a camel to go through the eye of a needle—a somewhat daunting observation for a biblical literalist.

He died a felon's death along with two thieves. His followers claimed that he rose again from the dead in three days. What happened to him then? A spurious text at the end of the Gospel of Mark tells us that he ascended into heaven, and the Apostles' Creed says the same. But the mood of the gospels seems to be that he simply went away. In all this we don't really see a personality that we can know with certainty. Albert Schweitzer wrote a book called, in English, *The Quest for the Historical Jesus,* and the quest goes on. Because we know so little, we can make Jesus almost anything we want. And what we have done for two thousand years is to make him the incarnation of our own values and to worship them and pretend that we are worshiping him.

Whom do we know in the New Testament? We know a little about Peter the fisherman but not much. The other disciples faded quickly into the haze of legend. The only person we know well in the entire New Testament is the Apostle Paul—and we don't like him. He has seldom been anybody's favorite saint.

We do know a lot of things that put us off. He was a Pharisee, a believer in resurrection against the Sadducees, a man converted dramatically on the Road to Damascus to the Christian teaching that resurrection is embodied in Christ. He speaks a lot about purity and condemnation, and he is an uncompromising believer in predestination. But he never speaks of hell. Death is the enemy—not eternal flame. He traveled. He was in jail far too often for a respectable institution like the Harvard Divinity School to consider him for a job, though it might—out of curiosity—have him in to lecture. He seems to have been a monomaniac in conversation, and we don't find him, as we find Christ, sitting down to dinner a lot. He was probably a fast-foods man.

He quarreled with Peter. "I withstood him to his face," Paul writes the Galatians, recalling the debate over whether Gentile converts to Christianity should be circumcised. It was Paul who commanded women to be silent in the churches, and it was Paul who proclaimed that man is the image of God but that woman is the image of man and that nature itself proclaims that it is an abomination for a man to have long hair. He is the least miraculous of all the saints—and, I repeat, we don't like him.

We never have liked him. The great churches of the Middle Ages were named for St. Peter, St. John, the Virgin Mary, occasionally for St. Stephen—seldom for Paul. London is an exception. The golden legend of Jacobus of Voragine spins marvelous yarns about St. Thomas, St. Lawrence, St. Bartholomew, the Virgin Mary, and legions of others. It treats Paul with circumspection. Many modern scholars have claimed that Paul ruined Christianity, that the faith started out as one thing and Paul wrenched it into another.

Poor man! Somehow I think he deserves better, but we know so much about him that we can't sickly over his hard, grim visage with the pale cast of legend. His image resists our reforming hand. To use one of his own metaphors, he is like a pot baked in the oven, and we can change only by breaking him. Legend says he was sickly; he speaks of a "thorn in the flesh." Certainly we can't see Paul sliding into second and knocking the second baseman into left field to break up the double play.

There is something just a little sad about Paul's fate. It does seem that the more we know anybody, the more we notice the flaws and the more we bring them up when the person's name comes up in our talk. I hasten to say that we ought to keep on the lookout for human failures so we can cry danger to those who may be deceived and damaged by them. Especially is this true in the civic realm.

But in the personal realm, I wish this and all communities could combine knowledge with charity and respect. It does seem that we take delight in seeing through people and then announcing the flaws we have seen, announcing them at the top of our voice. I find myself picking up books in my field to discover what I can to criticize, and a friend of mine speaks of the "bearable pain" one writer feels when he sees another get a bad review. Knowledge is our way of removing the armor of a foe and striking him. I wish we weren't that way. But I think of Jesus and Paul and reflect that human beings seem to give their deepest affection to those they can bend and mold according to their own comfort.

Cross Words

> Now from the sixth hour there was darkness over all the land unto the ninth hour.
> And about the ninth hour Jesus cried with a loud voice, saying, Eli, Eli, lama sabachthani? that is to say, My God! My God! Why hast thou forsaken me? (Matthew 27:45–46)

We have no sadder words in the Bible than these—the agonized cry of Jesus on the cross, a cry of loneliness and despair. They ring true. Rudolf Bultmann said that the one event certainly historical in the gospels is the crucifixion. No one creating a new religion would have invented a felon's shameful death for its founder and hero. The cross stands there in history, with Jesus

Delivered at Morning Prayers, Appleton Chapel, Memorial Church, Harvard University, 14 April 1995.

hanging on it, and from the moment it was hoisted aloft, Christians have been trying to explain it.

They have also done their best to pretty it up, and make the unbearable bearable to decent people like us who turn up in church on Good Friday to hear once again some idea of what it was all about.

It was not pretty. If Jesus was crucified outside of Jerusalem around Passover, it must have been a hot day, and the flies and gnats came in clouds to swarm on his wounds. He would have been crucified naked, without the modest covering of his private parts demanded by the fastidiously pious who commissioned paintings and sculptures of crucifixion in the medieval centuries and afterwards. He would not have been able to control his bowels and his bladder, and so crucifixion would have stunk, and the flies would have gathered there, too.

The Alexandrine Fathers of the third century pondered the nature of the incarnation and argued over the unpleasant possibility that Jesus possessed a fully functioning alimentary canal. Had they been witness to the crucifixion as it happened, they would have been rudely disabused of their elegant Platonism.

I've often thought that the worst part of crucifixion would have been those forcibly extended arms. It seems to be an almost universal gesture among monkeys, apes, and human beings that when we are threatened, we make a shelter of our hands and arms to hide behind. In the American Civil War, men charged into cannon and rifle fire with their arms shielding their faces as though they were walking into rain. To be spread-eagled in crucifixion robbed the victim of that elementary gesture of self-protection and left him helplessly exposed both to ridicule and to the indifferent curiosity of spectators who in all the ages quickly learn detachment from horrors not happening to them.

Crucifixion was a slow death by exposure that might take days. It is a mark against the traditional images of a strong, solidly build Jesus that he died within a few hours of being suspended on the cross. He must have been frail, perhaps even sick to die so quickly. And no choir sang *The Messiah*.

It was agony, the sort of thing the Romans were good at, and it was inflicted on the person Christians worshiped as the son of God, eventually as God Himself. This was a hard concept for early Christians—as it is for us. God suffer? One of the heresies of early Christianity was called "patripassianism," the notion that God the Father suffered in Jesus. The Greek fathers who gave us so much of our theology couldn't bear such a wild idea. Could God suffer pain, especially physical pain—almighty God, eternal spirit, maker of heaven and earth, holding past, present, and future in his hand? No, they said. A father God who suffered pain was not God.

The adoptionists tried to explain Jesus in this light. They said that Jesus was a human being somehow adopted by God, but at the crucifixion God departed before the first blow of the hammers that drove the nails into flesh. So God escaped pain. The poor, abandoned creature left there on the cross is pathetic indeed. And God in this view looks a little like Robert McNamara sedately retiring from the trauma of the Vietnam War to take his ease at the World Bank. It's not surprising that this theology never caught on.

We're simply left with a mystery. In the cross Christians somehow approach God through Christ, but that way is through the most appalling suffering and abandonment. If the idea of incarnation means anything, it means that our lives are like that. Yes, we have our feasts where we turn water into wine as Jesus did, following the example of Dionysus, the Greek god of wine and vitality and creation and even of sex. But there for all of us is also the cross, and life is like that.

Last year I heard Dale Evans speak at the Southern Literary Festival in Nashville. She is married to Roy Rogers. She sings, and she writes books about how sweet and particular Jesus is to her. She had just published another one. She turned her speech into an emotional testimony, her index finger lifted triumphantly towards heaven, as she told us in a trilling voice how Jesus had recently restored her from a heart attack so she could praise him for it this evening to us. Most gave her a standing ovation.

I sat there thinking, "It's nice that while all those thousands and thousands of people, including innocent children, are being massacred in Bosnia and in Rwanda that God looks after Dale Evans." And then I thought, "Someday even Dale Evans will die. And what then?"

Time magazine recently published a cover story about miracles. Most modern miracles are of healing. We don't get many floating ax heads or chariots of fire nowadays. We get spontaneous remissions of brain tumors. But even Lazarus, raised from the dead, eventually died. And when medical science finds a cure for cancer, we must still suffer and die—of something.

For the religious person, the greatest mystery is human suffering. We cannot explain it. We cannot avoid it. Religious charlatans, like Job's comforters, pander to the illusion that somehow we can escape suffering and death if we are only religious enough. But the most daring proclamation of the Christian faith is that Christ is Emanuel, God with us, not explaining suffering or relieving us of it or fleeing it, but suffering with us in pain, loneliness, shame, and death.

A Meditation on Creation and Time

And on the third day there was a
marriage in Cana of Galilee; and the
mother of Jesus was there:
And both Jesus was called, and
his disciples, to the marriage.
And when they wanted wine, the
mother of Jesus saith unto him, They
have no wine.
Jesus saith unto her, Woman,
what have I to do with thee? mine
hour is not yet come.

Delivered at Thomas Morus Gesellschaft, Mainz, Germany, 24 May 1995.

His mother saith unto the servants, Whatsoever he saith unto you,
do it.

And there were set there six
waterpots of stone, after the manner
of the purifying of the Jews, containing two or three firkins apiece.

Jesus saith unto them, Fill the
waterpots with water. And they filled
them up to the brim.

And he saith unto them, Draw out
now, and bear unto the governor of the
feast. And they bare it.

When the ruler of the feast had
tasted the water that was made wine,
and knew not whence it was: (but the
servants which drew the water knew;)
the governor of the feast called the
bridegroom.

And saith unto him, Every man
at the beginning doth set forth good
wine; and when men have well drunk,
then that which is worse: but thou
hast kept the good wine until now.

This beginning of miracles did
Jesus in Cana of Galilee, and manifested
forth his glory, and his disciples believed
on him. (John 2:1–11)

The tradition of the church ties this story from the mysterious
Fourth Gospel to the Eucharist, the changing of water into wine,
a miracle akin to the changing of the wine in the chalice to the
blood of Christ. But to the Hellenistic world of the Roman Empire
to which this story was first told, it would have immediately called
to memory the myth of Dionysus. Rudolf Bultmann tells us in his
commentary on the Fourth Gospel that devotees could leave ves-
sels of water in the temple of Dionysus and the god would change
the water into wine overnight. When Jesus did his miracle in a

moment, before the eyes of the servants, and in such quantity, he immediately proved himself superior to the pagan god.

But there is far more to this story than the mere victory of Christ over an inferior deity. The writer of the Fourth Gospel calls this miracle a "sign," and not only a "sign," but the *first* sign in the ministry of Jesus and therefore one of essential importance. So the writer invites us to see more here than the superficial details of a wonder that any magician might do.

Dionysus was not only the god of wine; he was also the god of life, of vitality itself, the god of creativity who caused children to be born and life to continue on earth. It is, therefore, of the first importance that this story comes soon after the sublime introduction of the gospel where we are assured that the same logos that created the world was also the divine force who created life and light. "In him was life," the gospel says, "and that life was the light of men." To gnostics living in the tortured world to which Christ came, human life in a physical cosmos was a prison house from which the soul should escape by denying itself all the physical pleasures and satisfactions. The physical world, said the gnostics, was created by a dark and evil god of matter who was opposed in cosmic warfare by an immaterial god of light who had no love for the physical. But here was Christ, the god both of light and of life in this world who was made flesh and dwelled among us. (The Greek text here tells us that he pitched his tabernacle among us.)

And in our text of the morning he attends a wedding and provides the wine that adds joy to the wedding feast. A wedding is the joining of husband and wife, making the two one flesh so that they not only cleave to one another but also produce children to propagate humankind to live in the world. So Jesus by his presence at a wedding affirmed the pleasure of God at our lives in a physical world, souls expressed by bodies sharing a beautiful earth and lifted to God by our experience of God's own creation.

As I have said, the god Dionysus was the god of wine and of the ecstasy that wine brings and of the ecstatic union with the living earth that we may experience in some forms of drunkenness. The followers of Dionysus gave themselves over at times to sexual orgies of drunken revelry where all restraint was forgotten in the bliss of the moment.

But here was Jesus acting the role of the god of life at a marriage where the bliss of wine and of procreation was restrained by the expectation that after tonight there would be tomorrow and that this year would be followed by a life and that at all times people are responsible to one another in the human community, not just for a moment but for all our days. A wedding, carried out publicly and by the conventions of the community where it takes place, is a formal agreement to be part of a world dedicated to orderly progression and renewal. A wedding is a sign that it is good to be alive and that it is good to bring more lives into God's beautiful world.

The wine that Jesus made is a sign of joy and not only a sign but God's own act in creating the source of joy in our physical being in time. We have enjoyed the physical pleasure of being together in these days. We have eaten and drunk, talked and listened, and some of us have sung, most of us in hymns in this morning worship and fewer of us in less divine songs late at night when we have lifted glasses and voices in simple merriment when the serious business of the day was done. I think that Thomas More, merry man that he was, would have loved all parts of our joy at being together. I think we honor him by our happiness in one another. I am moved always almost to tears by the plaintive words of his prayer composed in the Tower where he asked God to let him "be content to be solitary, not to long for worldly company."

He was a man born of friendship, and solitude was a deep and unnatural sorrow for him. Solitude was also an enemy to Martin Luther, who told his young disciples that they should flee solitude when they were melancholy, for when they were alone they had no power against the devil. We know that solitude has its virtues now and then, but we know also that to be merry in company is a gift of the god who has created us for the joy of one another, to love each other, to bear one another's burdens, and to help each other through time.

And that is the last lesson I have to draw from the text of the morning. A wedding is an affirmation of time. It betokens an agreement of a man and a woman to commit themselves to each other through an extension of moments that become days and years and a life set in a cycle of life where those who live and laugh and sing and cry today will, by a brief tomorrow, become pictures in fading photographs to be remembered only by name if by that, but the lives they create go on when they are forgotten by all but God.

It is akin to the view that Thomas More had of the place of the individual within the church, for he believed that faith was not some burning moment of mystical ecstasy that might, when it was done, leave the soul in ashes. To be a Christian was to belong to a community of the faithful that, though fearful and sometimes faint, extended in unbroken ranks from Christ through history to the ending of the world.

Christianity gained some benefits by the efforts of its early theologians to graft it onto Greek philosophy. But it also lost much. The Greek philosophers could not imagine a god subject to time. The Christian theologians who read the gospels through a Greek lens spent fruitless hours trying to reconcile the irreconcilable. Augustine worries through pages of his *Confessions* about how God could have spoken the words at the Baptism of Christ: "This is my beloved son in whom I am well pleased." To speak a sentence, said Augustine, means to make a beginning and to pass through time to an end. But how, he asked, is that possible to God, for whom all time is an eternal now, where past, present, and future are all one? Without knowing exactly what he was doing, I think, Augustine accepted a still and silent God, brooding over eternity.

And yet we know that we cannot be the beings we are without time. We are our memories. We will be now, in part, our memories of one another during this week, as some of us here are already, in part, the memories of one another through decades of time.

In his great poem "Sunday Morning," Wallace Stevens says twice, "Death is the mother of beauty." He means that our sublime sense of beauty comes from the fleeting sense of the moment, that the rising sun is moving towards full day, or that the magnificent stars are marching towards morning. Beauty lies in trying to grasp what is passing away.

Often we are all overwhelmed by our inability to make time stop and to hold to moments we would like to last forever. The Psalmist said, "As for man his days are as grass; as a flower of the field so he flourisheth; for the wind passeth over it, and it is gone, and the place thereof shall know it no more."

Yet we know that a moment that we cling to and hold turns beauty to dust. To watch the glorious sun stopped eternally at dawn would be to plunge the world into ice and fire, for life is in the motion, and motion and time are the same.

The story of the Fourth Gospel and the wedding in Cana where Jesus turned water into wine tells us that time is God's creation, given to us by his grace, to be used in joy and responsibility, and to be given up when by his providence it becomes our moment to let go.

The Eucharist comes to us as a physical proof that God's creation of the cosmos is good. The definition of transubstantiation at the Fourth Lateran Council in 1215 comes in a prologue to the decrees condemning the Cathars. The Cathars repeated the gnostic idea that the physical world was bad. Our text of the morning recalls the faith of the Eucharist that the world is good.

As Kant told us—long after the writer of the Fourth Gospel recognized this same truth—we cannot have a physical world without having time. We cannot escape time and space and still be the creatures God made us. We must accept both time and the world in the confident faith that they are good, that our part in them both—and with each other—is good, and that in the end all will be well.

Our lives within eternity are made up of days, all of them connected in the stream of time, yet all of them unique in that great river that Heraclitus tells us we can never step in twice. But as Christians we can sing always for every different moment the joyous song of the Psalmist, "This is a day that the Lord hath made; let us rejoice and be glad in it."

[Chartres Cathedral]

And it came to pass, that when
Jesus had finished these parables, he
departed thence.

And when he was come into his
own country, he taught them in their
synagogue, insomuch that they were
astonished and said, Whence hath this
man this wisdom, and these mighty
works?

Is not this the carpenter's son? Is
not his mother called Mary? and his
brethren James and Joses and Simon,
and Judas?

And his sisters, are they not all
with us? Whence then hath this man
all these things?

Delivered at Morning Prayers, Appleton Chapel, Memorial Church, Harvard
University, 5 February 1996.

> And they were offended in him.
> But Jesus said unto them, A prophet
> is not without honour, save in his own
> country, and in his own house.
> And he did not many mighty
> works there because of their unbelief.
> (Matthew 13:53–58)

At some point in most summers I throw a bicycle onto an airplane and fly to France and pedal for two or three weeks and in that time forget about the things I have not accomplished in the past year. Late last August I took my bike out of its box at Orly Field, south of Paris, put it together under the watchful eye of gendarmes watching for terrorist bombers, changed from long pants to short pants in the parking lot in front of the south terminal (the French pay no attention to flashes of middle-aged male nudity), and headed southwest.

Early the next afternoon I topped a long slope amid quiet fields and looked out to the familiar spires of Chartres Cathedral rising against the sky from about five miles away. I have been to Chartres many times, in my youth carrying a paperback copy of Henry Adams's *Mont St. Michel and Chartres* strapped to the luggage rack of my bike. Adams, having lost his own faith, turned with romantic nostalgia to the Middle Ages, the age of belief. He was one of many in the nineteenth century to see medieval Gothic as the summit of religious art. For many years I shared this romantic attachment and bicycled from one cathedral to another, thinking how fine it would be to have an unquestioned faith.

Later on Gothic began to make me uneasy. On this summer afternoon I bought an ice cream cone from a young woman at a stand before the great western portal. I asked her to watch my bike. I sat down on a stone bench, ate my ice cream, and looked up at carven epicene kings and prophets who stare out at the ages in unfaltering calm, radiant in the sun coasting down the summer sky. Gothic faces, whether in stained glass or in stone, possess an eternal tranquility. They suggest that it would be an insult to divinity to be astonished at any of the miracles they observe.

Inside the cathedral is a mosaic maze set in the floor, symbolizing the difficult path that Christian pilgrims must follow if they are to achieve paradise. A little girl, perhaps seven years old, wearing shiny patent leather shoes, was hopping on the maze, making it a game, completely absorbed in finding her way to the center. I stood watching her for a while, silently cheering her on, and I became aware of how the massive columns rose above us into the shadowy gloom of ogival arches and stained glass. She was so small, the cathedral so grand.

Like all Gothic cathedrals, Chartres is overpowering. The great French historian Georges Duby has pointed out that Gothic emphasizes royalty as well as religion. The kings of Judah whose carved stone effigies stand in ranks at most Gothic cathedrals gave to ordinary people a sacred idea of kingship itself. In the French Revolution, the mob pulled down the statues of these kings on Notre Dame of Paris and decapitated them. Gothic represented power. As Gothic rose in the twelfth century, the church sponsored crusades to slaughter Muslims in Palestine. Along the way the crusaders massacred Jews in the first great pogroms of Christian history. If war against the Turks proffered a ticket to heaven, why not practice by killing home-grown infidels, the helpless Jews who lived conveniently bundled in special areas in the cities of Christian Europe? Gothic also coincided with the beginning of the practice of burning heretics at the stake. "Heresy" means "choice" about what one believes, and medieval orthodoxy offered one choice—the official faith or death. Gothic may be taken as a statement in stone and glass not only of what we must believe but of the power to uphold the orthodoxy it represents—the power to raise an immense cathedral like Chartres and at the same time the power to crush dissent in blood and fire.

In one of those sudden, unexpected, and somewhat unwelcome revelations that come to us at times in life, I felt myself that afternoon in the camp of the enemy. I left the little girl hopping on the maze under the gargantuan and gloomy stone arches, reclaimed my bicycle, and pedaled on through recently harvested grain fields, glad to be back in the open sunshine.

Most religions raise gargantuan monuments. Only Saturday I read in the *New York Times* of a huge Southern Baptist church in my native Tennessee where visitors to the worship service are given an information sheet. It tells them that the sanctuary required ten thousand gallons of paint and one million square feet of sheetrock and that the church itself has twenty kitchens. Billy Graham held revival meetings in stadiums, and his henchmen gleefully quoted the size of the crowds as if numbers guaranteed authenticity.

Enormous professional football players now point their index fingers towards heaven after triumphant moments on the field. I thought they were signaling that they were number one. Then I read that they were pointing towards heaven to tell everybody in the stadium and the TV audience that God helped them catch that pass or score that touchdown or break the collar bone of that quarterback. I had no idea that God loved football so much.

Big buildings, big crowds, big success are proof to those who have them that God is with them. I'm reminded of a visit I made to a national monument called Massacre Rock in Idaho in 1973 while I was writing a novel about going west in 1851. I had become convinced by then that never in the history of the West did a wagon train circle up and fight off an Indian attack. But here was a Park Service monument to five whites killed by Sioux Indians in 1862 before the whites had time to circle their wagons. I was skeptical. I asked the young park ranger, "Are you sure this massacre really happened?" He looked at me blankly. "Why of course," he said, "why else would we have this park?"

Now here is a question. Does God really exist? I think lots of people say, "Why of course He exists; why else would we have this gigantic church?" "Of course He exists; why else would we have this crowd?" "Of course He exists; how else could I have sacked this quarterback?"

Against that background, our text of the morning is striking. Here is Jesus in his own country where everybody knows his family—his named brothers and his unnamed sisters, his mother, Joseph the carpenter. His neighbors evidently remembered him running around the village when he was a kid. We have no evidence at all that he had a distinguished appearance. He was likely short, swarthy, and thin, looking nothing at all like Charlton Heston. His neighbors found him insignificant because he was so much like themselves.

A few decades before the explosion of Gothic on the European landscape, the benign St. Anselm of Canterbury puzzled over how to define God. He said that God was that, greater than which nothing can be conceived. He did not say God is the greatest thing we can conceive; no, God is that than which nothing greater can be conceived. It's a curious, baffling definition. As Karl Barth suggested, it really means that no idea we shape of God on our own has any validity. God is greater than any of our conceptions about Him.

We assume that since God is great, He must be huge. But if the story of the incarnation means anything, it is that God comes to us on a human scale. The Jesus of the incarnation is elusive, mysterious, distant, and mediated to us by a fallible biblical text and a fallible tradition. But seen through the mists of time, one thing seems clear. Jesus is Emanuel, God with us, as the Sermon on the Mount holds, here among the least of these. If God is any-where, he is in the loud-mouthed, gap-toothed, homeless black man who sells *Spare Change* in Harvard Square. He is in the lonely, the despised, those who smell bad, the failure, and even in quarterbacks whose bones are broken by gargantuan Jesus freaks pointing index fingers towards the sky in jubilation. God is in failure, in defeat, in sickness, in the unjust suffering of the inno-cent, in age, and in death, and above all in the dark mystery of life that leaves us wondering what it means. We find no revelation in the starry universe nor in monuments we build to our religious conceits. We find revelation only in each other, and in doing what we can to find with the heart more than the eye can see.

The Wrestling Match

And Jacob was left alone; and
there wrestled a man with him until
the breaking of the day.

And when he saw that he prevailed not against him, he touched the
hollow of his thigh; and the hollow of
Jacob's thigh was out of joint, as he
wrestled with him.

And he said, Let me go, for the
day breaketh. And he said, I will not
let thee go, except thou bless me.

And he said unto him, What is
thy name? And he said, Jacob.

And he said, Thy name shall be
called no more Jacob, but Israel: for
as a prince hast thou power with God
and with men, and hast prevailed.

Delivered at Morning Prayers, Appleton Chapel, Memorial Church, Harvard University, date unknown. Published in *Harvard Divinity Bulletin* 28.1 (1998): 16.

> And Jacob asked him, and said,
> Tell me, I pray thee, thy name. And he
> said, Wherefore is it that thou dost
> ask after my name? And he blessed
> him there.
> And Jacob called the name of
> the place Peniel: for I have seen God
> face to face and my life is preserved.
> (Genesis 32:24–30)

This text is one of the more mysterious in the Bible. Jacob the patriarch, grandson of Abraham, is on his way to a meeting with his brother Esau. The two have not seen each other in years, not since Jacob cheated Esau out of the blessing of their father Isaac, causing Jacob to flee for his life from the anger of his wronged brother.

Jacob was anxious. He sent huge peace offerings ahead to Esau along with his two wives and numerous children while he himself remained behind, alone the Bible says, on the high banks of the river Jabbok that runs into the Jordan to the north of Palestine.

In that solitude and anxiety he encountered someone who wrestled with him all night long. The Bible says that the stranger could not prevail against Jacob, although he threw Jacob's hip out of joint. Still, Jacob held on until at dawn the stranger demanded to be released.

But Jacob was a capitalist when it came to blessing. He wanted as many of them as he could get. He refused to let go until his foe had blessed him. So the ghostly wrestler blessed Jacob, changed Jacob's name to Israel, and departed, refusing to tell his own name.

Jacob, obviously feeling triumphant over his victory, claimed he had seen God face to face and named the place Peniel, which means face of God. In his splendid book, *God: A Biography,* Jack Miles says that "Jacob's interpretation was not necessarily that of the author of the text"—a good point since Jacob is the Odysseus of the Hebrew Bible, tricky and deceitful. The Bible is somewhat more realistic than *The Odyssey,* showing us that, like most tricky and deceitful men, Jacob is deceived almost as often as he deceives others.

Miles suggests that maybe Esau was the night visitor, coming on Jacob to kill him in revenge for the trickery of years before. If Miles is right, the consequence was a double victory for Jacob. He won the wrestling match, and he alone could tell the tale. According to the code of nomad hospitality, Esau could not later admit to having tried to kill a brother coming in peace. Jacob took from the encounter a tall tale that he had wrestled not a man but God himself. Esau had to greet his brother with ostentatious forgiveness and remain silent while Jacob told his anecdote. As we all know, in the chase for celebrity, he who has the most anecdotes wins and gets the cover story in the *Sunday New York Times Magazine* or else a place in the Bible.

Of course, the whole episode may have been a dream. It did happen at night. We know that Freudians and other primitive peoples take dreams to be an extension of reality. We also know that both the Hebrew Bible and the New Testament are filled with dreams that God uses in much the same way that we use cellular telephones. We know, too, that Jacob had already been rung up by God through that medium. At Beth-el on his flight from Esau, he had seen the ladder extended from earth to heaven, thus giving centuries of children in summer camps something to sing about to keep from being afraid of the dark away from home.

True, Jacob did not represent this wrestling all night long as a dream. He said it really happened. But then he may have been mistaken, or he could have been up to his old tricky ways again, and he might have lied. If the wrestler was not Esau, we don't have any idea what his motive was. Why did he choose Jacob? Why that time? What did he want?

The only thing that seems clear in all this is that Jacob represented himself as wrestling with God, whom he claims to have seen face to face in the dark. I submit that, true or false, this is an astonishing claim. Here is a mortal claiming to have wrestled with the God who created heaven and earth with a few words, who destroyed the world with the hardest of all rains, and who poured molten sulfur down on Sodom and Gomorrah, reducing them to ashes and cinders. Not only does Jacob claim to have wrestled that God, but he also claims to have fought him to a draw, indeed to have pinned him until God made a deal with him to be let go before dawn. The claim seems almost blasphemous, or else the whole incident seems speciously staged to excite the masses as though in foretaste of televised matches by behemoths who belong to the World Wrestling Foundation. You or I would have trouble getting away with this yarn. But there it is.

Neither Jacob nor his family nor the rabbis who included the story when they assembled the book of Genesis thought of it as blasphemy. It was just another mysterious deed God had done. The God of the Bible does very odd things, including challenging Jacob to a wrestling match in the middle of the night.

I like what we see here. God's mysteries are sometimes painful; it is no fun to have your hip dislocated. The proper response is not to take all this lying down, not to say, well, that's just God acting up, and I'll have to accept it. The proper response is to fight back.

I have just completed a large book on Martin Luther, one of many in the history of religion who have taken an inherently nasty disposition and put it to work for God. Luther entered into one of the great debates of Western civilization with my personal hero of the Reformation, Desiderius Eramus of Rotterdam. Their topic was free will. Does God predestine us to salvation or re-demption? Or do we have at least some free will to determine our destiny? Luther argued that we have no choice, that we must be passive before God's almighty will. Erasmus objected, asking how we might expect mortals to be moral unless we have some choice in doing good or evil. Luther said in effect that God could not be God if human beings had free will; Erasmus said that human beings could not be human unless they could choose. The logic of divinity would seem to give the victory to Luther. But the real-ity of experience puts me on the side of Erasmus. I think the patriarch Jacob might well limp into this assembly, nursing his bad hip, to declare that he, too, was an Erasmian.

I do not believe in surrender to the inevitable. We wrestle in the dark with God almost every day. Like God against Jacob, we often find no motive in the forces that throw us about and seem to threaten our being and our dignity. I do not detect motive in ugliness, sorrow, anxiety, failure, depression, accident, cancer, or death. Nor do I detect motive in beauty, fame, fortune, good health, or a summa cum laude degree from Harvard—all those things that may have a hollowness at the core. Life comes at us as a succession of mysterious happenings where we are lamed and blessed and, like Jacob, defined. He got a new name, a new definition of himself, out of his night face to face with his dark foe. We rename ourselves with every struggle we have with pain and darkness, even the pain and darkness that, in this place called Harvard, can come from our victories. At every moment we have a terrible freedom to refuse to be resigned, to fight back against the iron weights in our souls that pull us down to apathy, to resist even the inertia of being so busy that we cannot consider who we are. Within human limitations we have choices even when it seems that we do not. We may emerge lame from the battle, but we may also win it, and it is a kind of victory if we make the struggle ours even if we lose.

[Psalm 139]

Oh Lord, thou hast searched me,
and known me.
Thou knowest my downsitting and
mine uprising, thou understandest my
thought afar off.
Thou compassest my path and my
lying down,
and art acquainted with all my ways.
For there is not a word in my
tongue, but, lo, O Lord, thou knowest
it altogether.
Thou hast beset me behind and
before, and laid thine hand upon me.
Such knowledge is too wonderful
for me; it is high, I cannot attain unto it.

From *An Affair of Honor* (New York: Alfred A. Knopf, Inc., 2001), 294–95.

Whither shall I go from thy
spirit? or whither shall I flee from
thy presence?

If I ascend up into heaven, thou
art there: if I make my bed in hell,
behold, thou art there.

If I take the wings of the morning and dwell in the uttermost parts
of the sea;

Even there shall thy hand lead
me, and thy right hand shall hold me.

If I say, Surely the darkness shall
cover me; even the night shall be light
about me.

Yea, the darkness hideth not from
thee; but the night shineth as the day:
the darkness and the light are both
alike to thee. (Psalm 139:1–12)

The verses I have read from the Psalms are filled with mystery.
They do not tell us what we would like to know. They tell us that
God knows us, our sitting down and our rising up, our thoughts
from afar, all our words and all our deeds. But they do not tell us
who or what God is. They do not tell us why the world is what it
is. They do not tell us why there must be suffering, why there
must be pain, grief, mystery, and death. . . .

I know that we do not know the answers to any of the questions that we all ask as we stand here. Why do children sicken
and die? Why do floods carry away the innocent? Why are tyrants
able to rage and kill? Why does war destroy millions who have no
desire to fight, no wish but to live in peace? Our Psalmist is clear.
We do not know, and anyone who presumes to give an answer
that claims to be God's word on the subject is a fool and a liar and
worst of all must be desperately deceiving himself. We yearn for
answers. So we make them up, and we say they come from God.
But they do not come from God, and we remain in ignorance.

Does even God have the answers? . . . My answer to that question . . . is that I do not know. How can we know? Has God spoken
to us? Has he revealed himself? He has not spoken to me. I do not

think he has spoken to you. Why then is God silent? There may be no answer to that question. Or maybe the answer is simply that God does not care for our world. Is that blasphemy? You may say so. But who has not had the thought? Another Psalmist pleaded with God, "Unto thee will I cry, O Lord my rock; be not silent to me; lest if thou be silent to me, I become like them that go down into the pit." Did God speak to him? We do not really know. And Jesus cried on the cross, "My God, my God, why hast thou forsaken me?" Was this a stage play? Was Jesus pretending the agony of loneliness in the universe? I do not think so.

We hope for a God like the God of the Psalmist, for whom the night shines like the day and who is to be found with us in the uttermost parts of our despair and ignorance. That is the best hope we can have, that if we make our bed in the grave God is there. If that hope is true—and we do not know that it is—our friend . . . is with God, and God is with him.

We do know this, that we are here, that we grieve, that we have lost a friend who was not like us, not like anyone else we knew. . . . We are in grief now. . . . [He] is at peace. That we know.

Let us pray. God, receive back to yourself this friend whom you gave to us, and let him and us be at rest. Amen.

Appendix
Ruleville: Reminiscence, Reflection

It can be worth your life these days to work for civil rights in Mississippi—and yet Mississippi is probably the most devoutly religious state in the nation. The irony of that paradox is embarrassing and enraging to dedicated churchmen. It is somewhat entertaining to those who believe that the church is a useless holdover from the past, eventually to be as extinct as the brontosaurus or the dodo bird, and the sooner the better. I believe that the origins of the paradox are enlightening in regard not only to the particular situation in Mississippi but to the situation of the church in the world.

Admittedly, my credentials for making these judgments are worn and perhaps blurred by time. Nine years ago [1954–55] I was attempting to be a ministerial student at the New Orleans

Baptist Theological Seminary. The essence of that school was evangelism, and each weekend a dedicated and zealous student body fanned out across the South in a frantic quest for souls. It fell to my lot to preach nearly every weekend for a year in Mississippi.

In many respects it was a grand experience. Everywhere I went, in every part of the state, the invisible phalanx of my office marched before me, opening doors of warmth and hospitality. Sometimes I slept in tenant farmhouses, equipped with three rooms and a path, and listened to the mice and rats scamper and chirp in the walls. At other times I slept in the neat little parsonages of more prosperous Baptist churches. Once I slept in a mansion in a great canopied bed from which I was wakened in the morning by a stout Negro maid who fearfully and reluctantly joined me in a solitary breakfast. I have eaten the best food of my life in Mississippi. And I have accompanied spirited men and howling dogs in nighttime hunts for fox and 'possum in the lonely woods.

In February of that year [1955] I went to Ruleville in the heart of the Mississippi Delta to preach in a weeklong revival. Ruleville was a small, drab place built around a shabby square. The white frame church where I preached stood in a grove of trees beside the road which ran from Ruleville to Cleveland. At some time in the past the foundations had settled, so the building tilted dangerously. But it stood fast, and it had stood in that precarious position for as long as anyone could remember; I suppose it is there to this day. The churchyard was part of a seven-thousand-acre plantation which lay close against the town. The owner possessed yet another gigantic holding elsewhere in the Delta. I never saw him, but the legends of his wealth hung over the town and soared upward into the rarefied regions of fantasy.

Near the church was the company store, managed by one of the members. Here the tenants, black and white, came to charge goods against their share of the crop and to have their purchases carefully noted in the large account book kept by the manager. The Negroes I met there were humble, terribly respectful. They seemed to know a hundred different ways to agree with a white man, and while they did so they would either smile and laugh, or shake their heads and look solemn, as if impressed by our marvelous wisdom.

Revival Meeting in Ruleville

The people who came to our revival were mostly white tenant farmers and their families. They were a pitiful lot—ragged, faded, tired. During that revival week the pastor, a student like myself, and I worked among them every day, all day long, preparing the harvest. We sat in tumbledown shacks where we could look out through cracks in the walls, and we tried to convince these people that Christ was the answer to all their problems. We believed that. And the revival was a success.

There is something awesome about the revival meeting in the South in which the preacher is carried away by his own words and the people are washed along in a lump behind him. In a secular, literary vein the prose of Thomas Wolfe or of William Faulkner comes as close to reproducing this word-frenzy of the southern preacher as anything I know. At the end of the sermon the pianist and the song leader catch the seething stream and turn it through the gates of some sentimental hymn like "Just as I Am" or "Softly and Tenderly," and the people are carried irresistibly to the front—often in tears, often shouting. It is a grand feeling, a kind of religious orgasm, akin certainly in effect if not in method to the ecstasy of Meister Eckhart or of John Tauler.

People wept in Ruleville, and they were converted, and the pastor and I felt as if we had seen God face to face. I do not know what has happened to that pastor in the years that have passed, but I wonder if he ever suspects that our great victory against the gates of hell was a cheap and ugly fraud.

Anyone now outside of Mississippi must wonder how the church there can stand its own shame and cowardice. But the issue transcends Mississippi and this crisis; it all comes down to the fundamental and agonizing question: Can the Christian church ever really serve men in a world like this? The churchman who looks south, over a new dark and bloody ground, must surely feel the tremor of John Donne's tolling bell.

When "Success" Means Failure

For in deepest reality the problems of the church in Mississippi are but warped and distorted reflections of the problems of the church in American society. The paradox posed in my opening sentence is an offshoot of the tragic paradox of church history; the most abysmal failures of the church grow out of its most ringing triumphs. In the case of Mississippi, the "success" of the church lies in the fact that it has responded to the needs of a great number of people with such effect that church and society have become almost indistinguishable. This is not quite the same thing as the *res publica Christiana* of the Middle Ages. But then it is not really so different.

In Mississippi, "society" is the white, Anglo-Saxon majority which has dominated the state from colonial times. The church through which this society expresses its religious concern is not one universal body but several churches—"churches" at least in name. There is, however, a "catholicity" in their conception of the nature of religion—emotional, often nearly orgiastic, devoid of real theological content, geared to the revival and the invitational hymn. This is the "catholic church" of Mississippi. Groups outside the "true church"—Jews, Catholics, often Episcopalians—are regarded with a grudging and suspicious toleration. Of the "in" groups the Baptists and the Methodists are the most important. But there is a vast array of smaller denominations holding to substantially the same principles, each vigorously contending that it practices the principles better than all the rest. As one would expect, the emotional aspects are somewhat subdued in such great churches as First Baptist of Jackson. But even there people hunger for a "great revival"—which really means an emotional religious outburst.

Now it may be—and surely is—argued by some that this kind of religion has not met the needs of Mississippians at all. Many seem to believe that what really has been needed in Ruleville is the ethical and intelligent monotheism of Yale Divinity School or Union Theological Seminary. But this is a little like arguing that what ninth-century Europe really needed was the brooding skepticism of Matthew Arnold or the urbane transcendentalism of

Channing or Emerson. Mississippi has its own problems, and in a way the church has met them.

When Hope Is Absent, Violence Is Present

What are these problems? They are the commonplaces of Ruleville—poverty, ignorance, a life that is usually nasty, brutish, and short. Around Ruleville, boundless and bare, the lone and level fields stretch far away. The vigorous and the intelligent get out of the desert. Periodically someone makes a survey of the state universities and colleges and announces in alarm that the vast majority of the students plan to leave Mississippi. For the enterprising and visionary laborers, northern industrial cities and relatives there beckon with promises of steady work and union wages. So they leave, to follow their neon stars. Those who remain are imprisoned within their flat horizons, turned over to a monotony of life without reward, without beauty or hope.

In such societies violence is never far beneath the surface. It provides a kind of escape. Faulkner raised Mississippi violence to an almost mystical background for existence. But to live in it is hell. Near another Mississippi town, I was told quietly and a little surreptitiously of a man who had been found shot to death on a country road, with his genitals burned off. He had had a reputation for chasing after married women, it was said. His murder had never been solved.

And there is always death. In Mississippi death strikes often through diseases which have been eliminated by the knowledge or merely the wealth of other parts of the country. It strikes through the accidents of machinery, of the "unloaded" gun, of storm and flood. And it comes through the violence of a casual cruelty, woven into the texture of society. Here the sophisticate may smile, but it seems to me that death is always more mysterious and more terrible in the lonely countryside, among the ignorant and the poor. In Mississippi death is a grave slashed in the soil and covered with flowers quickly wilted in the broiling sun. It is the ultimate seal of hopelessness.

Since it could not very well build a new life and a new people, the church has had to speak to people in the midst of this kind of life. Not too many people from the North did missionary work in the South before these latter days. And so the church in Mississippi has had to do the best it could with what resources it possessed. To the toiling poor, stricken by life, it proclaimed the nearness of God. For people obsessed with violence, it nourished a controlled violence of its own—the revival meeting with its incantational preaching, its intoxicating confessions, its blissful relief—all in churches lighted against the night in the nimbus of the vision of God. And over the graves of those who had had so very little in life the church threw its protective shadow, promising resurrection, golden streets, eternal song.

To return to my original point: In responding to desperate needs in Mississippi for simple comfort and for courage, the church has made its task horribly difficult in these times when, we cannot help but think, it should call down fire from heaven to devour the priests of Baal. Identified so closely with society, it is almost impossible for it to turn on that society and judge it. Its ministers are mostly natives, and beneath their titles and their pretensions they are human beings, oppressed and a little bewildered, as most human beings are, by the prospects of sudden and drastic change.

But beyond this is the fact that the church in Mississippi has become vital to the very understanding of the meaning of life. Therefore a congregation psychologically cannot permit its minister to deviate drastically from that set of values by which it comprehends itself. So the Mississippi preacher is not so free as is the northern university chaplain to sally forth to civil rights demonstrations and then return to his sanctuary, decorated with the trophies of his arrests—not, at least, if he wishes to continue to be a Mississippi preacher. He is not even as free as is the university personnel of his own state.

A Conscience for the Task of Repair

The dilemma brings us back to the question: is there any hope for the meaningful existence of the church in Mississippi—or anywhere?

The issue is not to be taken for granted. So far as we can see, the church is a human institution, and there is a certain inevitability about the demise of human forms. By faith we might say that the church is also divine and that it cannot pass away so long as the world stands. But that kind of declaration is more likely to provoke scorn than hope, and it smacks of a pride which might well go before destruction. Nevertheless, simply as an empirical human institution the church appears to be rooted too deeply in Mississippi society to be torn out. It will survive this crisis. And in the long run, that is something not to be despised.

In spite of its sins, the church has laid the groundwork for a Christian conscience in Mississippi. An appeal to that conscience does mean something; until now it has not been turned toward race, but the change is coming. It has already taken place in the seminaries. Whatever may be their uneasiness or their restrictions, the young men graduating and going into Ruleville or Cleveland or New Albany or Walthal are becoming more uneasy and more restricted when they seek to justify the racial practice of their society.

It will take time for appeals to this Christian conscience to have real effect. And there is no doubt that other forces will run ahead of the church. This will not be the first time—nor the last—that the church, moving like some sluggish battleship with a damaged rudder, has turned slowly and ponderously to follow in the wake of the swifter and the more daring. But the church has finally carried its people with it.

Long after the legal battles have been won and the Negro has achieved equality in education and economics, a broken society will need to be put together again. No institution in the South will be in a better position than the church to work at this task of repair. It might even be said that if the church does not do this job, it will not be done at all. This too will be a slow process;

progress from year to year will not be spectacular, and it is not certain that it will take place at all. But the church, while never succeeding very well in its crusades, has succeeded in its power to mend and to heal. The true prophet is always dissatisfied with this role; if he were not, he would not be a prophet. Society being what it is, however, it needs both the prophet to show the way and the plodding institution to follow him from afar.

And so, I think, we must be of two minds about the church in Ruleville—or wherever it may be, in the South or perhaps in the world. As moral beings and as Christians, we must judge it both theologically and ethically for what it has not done. But at the same time we cannot afford to wash our hands of a bad business and dismiss from serious consideration the potential contribution of this vast institution, so powerful and yet so weak. Even in that Baptist church at Ruleville there are planted quiet seeds of redemption and an earthly kind of resurrection. The progress of the church in Mississippi may seem so imperceptible as to lead us to think that it does not move at all. Certainly the brave young people now laboring there must think that. *Eppur si muove.* Nevertheless, it does move.

Wrestling with God was designed and typeset on a Macintosh computer system using QuarkXPress software. The body text is set in 9.75/13 Berkeley and display type is set in Cheltenham. This book was designed and typeset by Kelly Gray and manufactured by Thomson-Shore, Inc.